## What Critics and Readers are Saying

. . . for Christians dealing with the challenges of mental illness in their spouse, this is **a must-read.**

*— BlueInk Reviews, starred review*

. . . empathetic . . . relatable . . . practical . . . **a warm, inviting faith-based self-help guide** for married couples seeking to understand and overcome their respective challenges and remain together.

*— BookLife Review*

. . . **highly recommended** . . . neatly wound into Christian beliefs in a way that psychological perspectives alone can't fully address.

*— Midwest Book Review*

What a **profoundly helpful and moving** book! . . . full of hope and wisdom for any marriage in an easy-to-read format. . . practical, spiritually sound recommendations. The author and his wife's transparent stories of their struggles provide **rare windows into the complexity of these challenges** and illustrate how spouses can rise above through Christ. **Highly recommended.**

*— Robert Reich, synod leader and pastor*

**So thrilled that a book like this is available.** Coupling marriage and mental health, with a lens of faith, is a gift for newlyweds to forty-year partners.

*— Ganel-Lyn Condie, bestselling author,*
*video host, suicide prevention advocate*

*Healing the Stormy Marriage* **opened my eyes** about ways to improve my own marriage of 41 years! I have not seen any other book that addresses mental illness, marriage, and relationships with so much hope and practical advice. . . The book is respectful and balanced. The format was especially helpful to me for referring back to key passages, charts, and points. I found the Scripture references accurate and doctrinally sound. . . It was lively and kept me wanting to read . . . **This book fills an important need!**

> — *Mardi, reader*

**I like the way it's written—straightforward but kind.** I feel supported reading it. . . I think it will help many couples.

> — *Kendra, reader*

. . . a **fresh approach with an inspirational perspective** to a multitude of issues in marriages. Don't all of us need help to some degree?

> — *Margaret, reader*

*Happy After All* . . . offers a **wide variety of tools and practices** that will allow you to pursue health as an individual and a couple.

> — *Emily Louis, Abundant Grace podcast*

# HEALING THE STORMY
# MARRIAGE

# HEALING THE STORMY
# MARRIAGE

## Hope and Help for YOU
### when Your Loved One has Mental Health or Addiction Issues

## R. CHRISTIAN BOHLEN
### WITH HELEN M. BOHLEN

Carpenter's Son Publishing

Published by Carpenter's Son Publishing, Franklin, Tennessee. Published in association with Larry Carpenter of Christian Book Services, LLC. www.christianbookservices.com

Scripture quotations marked (NIV) are taken from the Holy Bible, New International Version®, NIV®. Copyright © 1973, 1978, 1984, 2011 by Biblica, Inc.™ Used by permission of Zondervan. All rights reserved worldwide. www.zondervan.com The "NIV" and "New International Version" are trademarks registered in the United States Patent and Trademark Office by Biblica, Inc.™

Scripture is used from the New King James Version, © 1982 by Thomas Nelson, Inc. All rights reserved. Used by permission.

Holy Bible, New Living Translation, copyright © 1996, 2004, 2007 by Tyndale House Foundation. Used by permission of Tyndale House Publishers, Inc., Carol Stream, Illinois.

Scripture is used from the English Standard Version, © 2001, 2007 by Crossway Bibles, Wheaton IL, All rights reserved. Used by permission. www.esv.org/.

Edited by Michele Preisendorf of Angela Eschler and Associates
Cover Design by Brian Halley
Interior Layout Design by Adept Content Solutions
Ebook Layout Design by Marny K. Parkin

Printed in the United States of America

First Softcover Edition: November 2, 2021

ISBN: 978-1-949572-77-3

Another book by R. Christian Bohlen:

**Jesus Christ, His Life and Mine: The Story of Jesus and How It Applies to Us in the Twitter Era**

Learn more:

# Contents

**Disclaimer**: Readers and their spouses are advised to seek professional diagnoses and personalized recommendations from qualified mental health professionals. This book is not a substitute for medical care from credentialed professionals. Recommendations in this book are not to be construed as instruction, direction, or prescriptive, medical advice.

If you suspect that a mental illness or disorder may be present, it is very important that you encourage your spouse to meet with a qualified mental health professional. Whether or not you have been able to meet with a mental health professional, this book can help you develop strong, healthy foundational habits for self-care and a healthy marriage.

**Caution**: If at any point your spouse is demonstrating any self-harming behaviors or mentioning thoughts of self-harm or suicide, seek emergency medical care by calling 911. Never be afraid to take such action if there is serious concern about their safety.

# A New Destination

*Circumstance,*
*Which HURT me cruelly,*
*Crept in without invitation.*

*The frightening guest,*
*A monster it seemed,*
*Made OUR home its habitation.*

*Though I failed to evict,*
*Great PEACE became mine*
*Through choice and inspiration.*

*Correct knowledge was key,*
*More so, power from GOD.*
*We have hope in a new destination!*

—R. Christian Bohlen

# Introduction

Imagine you just moved to a new city. Within days, you become friends with a neighbor—a talkative, energetic woman who makes you laugh and feel loved and accepted.

Soon, your new friend begins sharing more about her life situation. She is separated from her husband for the fourth time. She says she loves him deeply, but he never gives her the unconditional love she deserves. And now he left her here all alone—but this time he's intent on divorce.

Days later, she lets it all out with surprising transparency. She's been in and out of mental hospitals with occasional suicide attempts. She says her husband wants her to be perfect and she'll never live up to his expectations. She admits freely to fighting with him and yelling "more than she should" and having some impulsive, addictive behaviors. She takes medications sometimes, but she's convinced the doctors don't understand her and "they always take sides with her husband," even though her husband of fifteen years has a diagnosed mental condition himself and now claims to have PTSD because of her!

"We prayed about our marriage beforehand," she tells you. "I guess my husband just doesn't trust God enough to stay with me. And he was so cold when I last saw him. It was like he never even loved me."

She then stops, raises her head, and looks at you with anguished eyes and asks, "Do you think we have a chance of surviving as a couple?"

\* \* \*

Honestly, what would you think about the chance of your new friend's marriage coming together again and happily enduring through the rest of their lives? Dismal? A tiny chance?

Most would think this is a hopeless case. But in truth, the couple described above is *us*, the authors of this book.

## The Secret

Congratulations on your decision to care for and pamper yourself by reading this book. You absolutely deserve it. You are not alone, nor is your situation anything to be ashamed of. From the American Psychiatric Association:

> *Mental illness is common. In a given year, nearly one in five (19 percent) U.S. adults experience some form of mental illness.*[1]

And would you have imagined this astonishing statistic could be true?

> *In the United States, almost half of adults (46.4 percent) will experience a mental illness during their lifetime.*[2]

Most adults with mental illness are in a close relationship with a loved one—someone like you. This book is specifically for *you, their spouse*.

Like you, many spouses of mentally or emotionally unstable loved ones are under incredible stress. Often, such marriages crumble because the so-called "spouse who has fewer challenges" crumbles. They see no way out but to get out. But there is another way:

> 💡 If spouses of the mentally ill or addicted can be spiritually strengthened and learn practical things they can do independently, more marriages can be saved.

If there *is* a secret to saving such challenging marriages, that is it.

## How to Read This Book

Feel free to jump to any chapter or topic that meets your needs. We do recommend reading the short but essential chapter 1 first, but after that, skip around to your heart's content.

Because circumstances can vary significantly from couple to couple, and because, depending on your personal circumstances, there are things presented that could be upsetting or triggering for your spouse—like chapter 4, "Can I Survive This?"—we typically recommend you not read this book as a couple.

Let this book be your getaway and your means of strengthening yourself. After you read in private and have a better feel for what may or may not apply to your situation, you may choose to discuss the things you've learned with your spouse.

## Seeking Professional Help

Your spouse need not have been diagnosed for you to benefit from this book.

💡 If you suspect a mental illness or disorder, your spouse (and/or you) should meet with qualified mental health professionals. This book cannot replace such essential care.

But while awaiting or after receiving a diagnosis, this book can help you tremendously in developing foundational habits.

## About the Authors

I, Christian, am the author of this book in terms of putting the words on paper and writing from the spouse's perspective. But this book contains the important contributions of my wife, Helen. In fact, the idea for this book started with my wife, who became aware that there are not many resources available to the *spouses* of those with serious mental, emotional, and/or addiction issues.

We are deeply grateful we were able to "hang in there" and not give up. We each have multiple diagnosed mental illnesses. Yet we are "happy after all" in our thirty-fifth year of marriage and believe God has given us special experiences and backgrounds to be able to help others.

We are not mental health experts. However, the marriage and mental health recommendations set forth in these chapters are based on solid research and advocated by respected professionals. Be sure to visit appendix B, "Recommended Reading," which points you to free online resources and six terrific books we strongly recommend.

We *are* experts, however, in how to find increasing happiness despite overwhelming odds. You'll find many of our stories sprinkled alongside the science and professional recommendations. Plus, you can read our more detailed story in appendix A, "Our Story." In fact, if you want to understand our experiences first, feel free to jump there now.

## Healing and Happiness

You've likely asked yourself, "Can we ever be happy after all we've been through?" That's what this book is about—helping you answer and achieve that. Note that our view of happiness is based on scripture, which usually refers to it as "joy."

> Healing and joy come when we believe, embrace, and humbly align ourselves with God's plan for our lives as opposed to resisting or angrily rebelling against Him.

We believe spouses can experience greater healing and joy when they strive to believe in and follow Jesus Christ. Marriages with mental health and addiction issues cry out, *scream*, even, for the divine help and healing God's grace provides.

We hope you have already discovered or are at least open to Jesus Christ as a source of strength in your life. In most chapters, we include Bible scriptures, principles, and stories that promote healing and wise decision-making.

We testify and even celebrate the truth that gospel peace and joy can exist amid pain. They do not require the elimination of pain.

Our life is rich and generally peaceful now. There are joy and understanding beyond words. We lie not, nor do we exaggerate. Thank God in heaven our marriage is preserved as two souls in love. And we credit the teachings of the Bible and mental health professionals as captured in these pages.

## A Warning

A warning is in order, however. Studying this book without applying the principles found herein has little value. Happiness can escape us even as we hold the answers in our hands. As best-selling authors

Francis and Lisa Chan soberly observed, *"Christians in America have become experts at conviction—and failures at action."*[3]

We promise your healing can be dramatic and, in some ways, instant, but that requires a soft, pliable, believing, humble heart.

Even though you can find healing and direction, neither this book nor any other can promise that your relationship will improve and survive. The unavoidable truth is that some marriages are destructive. These tragic, complex situations are discussed in chapter 4, "Can I Survive This?"

## Our Backgrounds

It may help if we share a bit about our backgrounds to illustrate our own mental health issues and strugglings with spiritual darkness.

### Christian's Background

God must have smiled with compassion when He designed my family's life. My dear mother suffered from anxiety much of her life. She was hospitalized for a month with a nervous breakdown during the 1950s, which many consider the dark ages of the psychiatric profession. Though based on good intentions, her "treatment" nearly destroyed her and almost prevented her from becoming my mother. But with faith in Christ and patience to accept her ongoing challenges, she emerged victorious and today is generally healthy and always cheerful.

My father almost certainly had a mild form of depression. His father was also likely depressed, became an alcoholic, and died rather young.

My brother was a brilliant and charming individual, among the top in his high school class and an outstanding science student in college. Suddenly, he started acting strangely. Within three years, his behavior became so bizarre my parents realized something was very wrong. He was diagnosed with schizophrenia, which means "separated from reality." My brother suffered in the extreme, with multiple suicide attempts, hospitalizations, experimentation with medications that worked poorly, and little enjoyment in life. He lived in a group home and still acted oddly until he died—even with the more advanced medications available today. He passed away from COVID-19 in 2021.

I have a form of bipolar disorder known as bipolar disorder 2, which is often misdiagnosed as "clinical depression." Typical antidepressants don't work for bipolar 2, and it took years for doctors to correctly diagnose me and find medications that worked. My medications now work spectacularly, and I feel amazing and healthy.

I'm also open about the fact that I'm a recovering drug addict. Many years ago, I got caught up in an illegal lifestyle and heavily used drugs that were difficult for me to give up. I credit the saving power of Jesus Christ in changing my heart and freeing me from the desire to use drugs.

Faith in God didn't come naturally to me. I experienced a major crisis of faith in my twenties but emerged with an unforgettable experience and the ability to truly connect to the light of Jesus.[4]

## Helen's Background

My wife's family experienced dysfunction and turmoil that deeply affected them all. Her father and mother stayed married through a great deal of struggle. They were lovely people who became positive influences on us in our later years, which illustrates how God works in His children over time to draw them closer to Him, if they will let Him.

Helen's childhood is almost completely devoid of memories except for the summer camps for kids with disabilities she attended for a whole month every year from age eight to sixteen. (Helen was born with her left leg paralyzed from the knee down and required a leg brace to walk. Thanks to dozens of surgeries on her foot and legs, her ability to walk improved but today she typically uses a wheelchair.)

To this day she vividly remembers funny stories about the summer camp activities, pranks, other kids she loved, and her college-aged counselors. But her memories of home life are largely missing, which she finds strange and unsettling. Her doctors strongly suspect childhood abuse.

She recalls being a "model child" at home and believes she obeyed her parents until she reached age sixteen, when she increasingly came to loggerheads with them. Following one particularly bad fight, at age seventeen, she moved out of her parents' home and into the home of her boyfriend's family. Her relationship with her parents returned to normal by the time we were dating.

She was married for three years before we met. I later learned her first marriage was marred by constant fighting.

Helen has always been kindhearted toward the underdog and a friend to the geeks and weirdos around her (which explains how we ended up together!). But faith in God was never important until she reached her twenties. Even then, her commitment to God was off and on, and she struggled with addiction from time to time.

## Professional Experience with Abnormal Behaviors

Shortly after my wife and I married, I started working at a drug and alcohol rehabilitation facility for court-committed juvenile males in northwest Pennsylvania. They ranged from rural pranksters and pot smokers to drug dealers, gang members, and killers. I'm convinced it was a heaven-sent opportunity for me to help others while helping myself.

I was a schoolteacher to the young men in that facility, but I was also involved in clinical discussions about their behavior and mental health. Through my own graduate-school studies as well as work-related training, I learned a great deal about human learning, abnormal psychology, sociology, and criminology, which greatly expanded my understanding of the human condition and the depth of suffering that exists in our fallen world.

It was at that juvenile facility, ironically, that I truly recovered from my own addiction and "grew up." To this day, I love the Hindu proverb that aptly describes what I experienced while helping those young men—as well the growth I experienced while striving to support my spouse:

*Help your brother's boat across and see!*

*Your own has reached the shore!*[5]

## Chapter 1

# I'm So Confused

After all you've been through, you're probably craving relief from confusing thoughts and feelings like these:

*"I'm afraid of what might happen today."*

*"Who is this person I married? I don't know him anymore."*

*"Why are my efforts never good enough?"*

*"How much of this is my fault (like she says it is)?"*

*"Why can't she handle even a little stress, like I can?"*

*"Sometimes he talks in circles and makes no sense at all."*

*"I feel stuck inside this terrifying, emotional roller coaster."*

*"I can't hide this from other people anymore . . . but I'm so embarrassed."*

*"Why aren't my prayers working? Doesn't God see all this?"*

*"I'm starting to question everything I ever believed."*

Please know how much we empathize with you! We wish we could see you and look into your eyes. You deserve all the heartfelt love and compassion we can offer. We promise, you will feel it in these pages.

So many struggle with challenges similar to yours. Many suffer until they can't stand it anymore and give up. But you have made the decision to explore options that can make a difference. Your wise choice will pay off. But how?

**1**

You'll be happy to know that finding initial relief from your confusion doesn't require your spouse to change. You can experience increasing clarity by learning and doing certain things independently. What a stress-relieving, empowering thought! You are in control, and this book will show you how to apply that control for your benefit and blessing.

Your confusion will diminish as you learn about and apply each of the following in your life and relationship:

1. The power of God
2. Principles that lead to a happy marriage
3. The nature of your spouse's condition and how best to deal with it

> 💡 This book takes the position that lasting progress in your relationship requires learning and action in each of the above areas.

## Why All Three?

It's easy for us to forget that our spouses comprise much more than their mental or emotional issues. You may be used to focusing on their confusing jumble of mixed messages and erratic behaviors, but our spouses also have healthy, valuable, and delightful attributes.

It's harmful and shortsighted to think of your spouse only in terms of their unhealthy condition(s). You and your spouse each have unique and "normal" talents, preferences, personalities, etc.

Even so-called healthy spouses are a bit wacky, making this lovely quote ring true for most of us: *We are all a little weird. . . . When we find someone whose weirdness is compatible with ours, we join up with them and fall in mutual weirdness and call it love.*[1]

We begin improving our relationship as soon as we begin viewing it holistically to include 1) the needs of the soul, 2) the typical needs of the marriage relationship, and 3) the unique challenges that accompany mental, emotional, or addiction issues.

Consider the needs of the soul for a moment. From a biblical perspective, we each have a spirit.

*But there is a spirit in man: and the inspiration of the Almighty giveth them understanding. (Job 32:8)*

In both your life and your spouse's, spiritual vision and understanding are darkened to a degree because we live in a fallen world and we sin in various ways (see Romans 5:12). Therefore, some of us have embraced and reflect more of God's light, and some are more attached to Satan's ways and darkness.

Why point this out? Because spiritual darkness adds yet another layer of challenge and confusion to your marriage. When we do not accept or live by the light of God's word, we are—according to scripture—in the bondage of sin. We're stuck in our selfishness.

This means *us*, not only our spouse (see John 8:31–36). It is as if a mist of darkness partially veils our perception and taints the way we act (see 2 Corinthians 4:4 and 1 John 2:11). Such darkness is not the *only* destructive force in a marriage but it can be a major one that is overlooked.

As Denis de Rougemont put it, *"Why should neurotic, selfish, immature people suddenly become angels when they fall in love?"*[2]

We don't become instant angels when we marry, do we? Sin and selfishness follow us into marriage. But deep spiritual change through Jesus Christ helps us rise out of the darkness in our lives, making it easier to interact peacefully and progress in our relationships.

## God Sees Us Entirely—Past, Present, and Future

As spouses, we cannot clearly see why our mate is acting the way they do. Is it because they are selfish and stubborn? Is it because they have underdeveloped relationship skills and quite literally don't know any better? Is it because of their mental condition?

You and I cannot judge. But know this: God knows the root cause of their behavior. God knows what is possible given your spouse's circumstance. God sees your spouse's spiritual potential and their future willingness to change and deal with their mental health or addiction issues. This is why making it a priority to rely on God's power and guidance is the number-one recommendation of this book.

> ◆ Only God fully understands what is going on in your relationship now and what it can become in the future. He can guide you.

## You: The "Seeking" Spouse

In reality, nearly all marriages involve two spouses who have varying degrees of mental, emotional, or spiritual issues and unhealthiness. You may feel this is untrue or even unfair. We ask that you be open to this important point: neither spouse in your marriage is the good guy or the bad guy, the healthy one or the unhealthy one. One of you may have greater challenges and disruptive behaviors than the other, that's true.

But how shall we think of you versus your spouse? Surely, calling you the "healthy spouse" would be an oversimplification.

Perhaps it's more accurate to think of you as the "seeking spouse."

You are seeking relief from confusion and pain, correct? You seek guidance. You seek strength and inspiration from God. You are rightly seeking all of these important and positive things. Yet you likely also have issues and challenges contributing to the stressful dynamic in your marriage. As you seek solutions, please be on the lookout for personal issues that may require you to seek professional support and change.

# Chapter 2

# How Can I Start Feeling Like Myself Again?

**M**y life and health were severely affected by my wife's disorders. Within two years of our marriage, I was seeing a licensed psychologist seeking guidance and relief. Some years later, I was diagnosed with post-traumatic stress disorder (PTSD), just like soldiers in a war zone, although my war zone was the chaos of our marriage. I couldn't believe it. But the diagnosis did make sense, and my symptoms matched. And I *had* been through an excruciating war on my psyche and senses.

My hopes for a peaceful relationship and my tender efforts to be a good spouse were being blown to bits. I started to seriously doubt nearly everything I had ever understood or believed about who I was and what marriage could be like. I became jumpy, easily frightened, and was always waiting for the next battle. Deepening depression sapped me of energy and smothered my ability to function normally and feel joy. But I still had to go to work every morning. I still had to try and cope with my wife's struggles.

## What's Happening to Me?

It's common for spouses of challenging, unstable partners to feel like they themselves are changing in ways they don't understand.

So, how can you start feeling normal and feel like yourself again?

Let's start by understanding the nature of what you're going through. The disturbances from our spouses and the unpleasant effects on us come in three flavors, like vanilla, chocolate and twist:

**5**

1.  Extreme or erratic emotions
2.  Nonsensical perceptions, ideas, words, and actions
3.  Both extreme/erratic feelings and nonsensical communication in the same episode

Your spouse's illness has probably served up generous helpings of all three flavors. Mine did. But I did recover, feeling better and stronger than ever, and we are confident you can too.

## Feelings Happen . . . Now What?

Let's take a close look at that first flavor of disruption you've been served: extreme or erratic emotions.

How do you think any rational person would react if they lived with someone exhibiting one or more of the behaviors listed below? Would you fault them if they felt frustration, fear, or anger?

- Angry outbursts, sometimes for long periods
- Overreactions to mildly stressful situations
- Intense fears, thrashing or hitting during nightmares
- Rapidly changing moods (e.g., from sobbing to laughing)
- Frequent somber, withdrawn behavior
- Lack of interest in anything, including fulfilling responsibilities

Anyone would have an emotional response when experiencing these behaviors from someone they love. *Anyone.* It is normal and unavoidable. You have surely felt fearful, angry, frustrated, hurt, ashamed, accused, guilty, powerless, unloved, impatient, panicked, and more.

> 💡 Grant yourself this gift today: believe that feelings are okay. Once they start flowing, they should not be suppressed. Feel them and let them flow out of you.

The wise, healthy response is to allow yourself to feel even unpleasant feelings. But that doesn't mean you have to act on those feelings. Feeling and acting on feelings are two very different things.

- Feeling impatient doesn't mean you have to make that nasty remark.
- Feeling angry doesn't mean you have to curse or hit.

- Feeling unloved doesn't mean you have to lecture your spouse about all the ways they have been unkind to you.

Feelings flow like a river. You can't dam them up. There is a never-ending wellspring of conscious and unconscious emotion that feeds your feelings.

Photo by Esa Hitula

Whether because of your interpretation of scripture or your expectations for yourself, you may have tried to stop them from flowing. But that doesn't work in the long run. The emotional waters keep flowing in. If you try to dam them up, you run out of fingers and hands and toes to plug the holes as the waters keep spilling over and through your dam. Ultimately, you *will* feel them in one way or another.

If we have been severely and constantly mistreated, our emotions can swell into confusion and rage. [1] They become like hungry dogs in the basement who won't settle down until they are released. Ignoring them or telling ourselves we must be evil because the angry dogs keep barking is not going to work, nor is it healthy. Do not tell yourself you are evil because of negative thoughts or overwhelming and unmanageable feelings. Seek help from a qualified mental health professional.

Also, chapter 7, "I'm Totally Drained and Afraid" will show you how God can help you bear the painful situations you face.

## Emotional Self-Abuse

Emotional abuse is very real and painful. You may be experiencing it from your spouse already. But have you ever considered that by not allowing yourself to truly feel your feelings, you're unwittingly abusing yourself?

When inflicted upon us by another person, emotional abuse aims to "diminish another person's sense of identity, dignity and self-worth."[2]

Whenever I hid from my own feelings or tried to squash them, my "sense of identity, dignity and self-worth" evaporated. I did to myself what abusers do to their victims.

And then where was I? I had turned into someone I didn't recognize. I had lost who I was because my emotions had been demoted to a swirl of hidden forces deep within me—but never gone.

> 💡 Your emotions are a big part of who you are. You can't disconnect your heart and put it in a jar for safekeeping and expect to feel well.

If this seems far-fetched, we invite you to research the dangers of suppressing your emotions. There's even a severe form of it diagnosed as emotional detachment disorder (EDD). The physical effects of emotional detachment are significant, including memory issues, high blood pressure, obesity, digestive issues, fibromyalgia, frequent illness due to a suppressed immune system, and more.

*Studies have shown that repressed emotion can be linked to a wide range of physical and mental health complications in the long run.*[3]

## How to Feel Your Feelings

How do we get back to our true selves—our natural childlike state of being authentic with what we feel and free of guilt?

It may seem silly to have a section in this book called "How to Feel Your Feelings." It's not. You may even need professional help to get in touch with your feelings again. But you may be able to make progress as simply as this:

1. When you suspect that your emotional river is starting to rise, name the feeling in your mind. "I feel angry," "I feel disappointed," "I feel frustrated," or whatever it is, and then say to yourself, "And that's okay."
2. Allow yourself to feel the swell of anger or disappointment or frustration come in. Notice it, acknowledge it, accept it, and then finally let it flow right out of you. The energy will flow out of you once you feel it. The act of acknowledging it and feeling it without judgment or repression constitutes "feeling it." It's done at that point. You felt it. The energy has passed through you.
3. Practice feeling pleasant feelings in the same manner. When you are relieved, relaxed, or enjoying a laugh, feel it more deeply than usual. Notice it. Enjoy it as long as you'd like.
4. Notice when you physically exhale in relief, like "Ahhh." Often, this involuntary physical reaction accompanies the simple act of feeling the emotional waves that are part of you.

In crisis situations, feelings quickly come from every direction. Learning to feel and let those feelings flow out of you takes time and requires reasonably calm situations in which to practice and build confidence. Eventually, even explosive situations will not overwhelm you. If you are regularly exposed to crises and extreme emotions, you will certainly need support from a mental health professional.

### Helen's Perspective

[How she felt years ago]: I don't like it when Christian starts talking about himself and how he feels. It makes me nervous. I already know I'm not good for him, and then when he tells me he feels hurt and mentions what I've done wrong in any way, it scares me and makes me feel guilty. It's always my fault. So I don't want to talk about his feelings. I'm the one who needs help and understanding. Let's just leave him out of this.

When I feel a little more emotionally stable and my meds are working, I can handle it a little better, but I still don't like it. What he is really saying is that he wants me to do something different. I never feel like I can be successful when somebody tells me I have to do something different, so it feels like I'm being set up for divorce.

Even when he tries to say what he is feeling in the way our mental health coaches tell us to, like "I feel (such and such) when (such and such) happens," it still feels like a finger-pointing session. Just because he doesn't say "you," doesn't mean I'm not at fault. I still started it, he's saying, and that scares me. I'm the problem. I'm always the problem.

[Fast-forward twenty-seven years with effective meds and therapy]: I gradually learned how to recognize my own fears and let Christian express his feelings. I'm still not good at it when he just blurts things and sounds mean, but even then I can separate "him" from "me," and I know he needs to feel and express himself. I couldn't understand or accept that years ago. I just didn't have it in me, and no amount of him begging or lecturing me could get me to understand it. I just got more scared and angry. We now talk openly about our feelings, and we are both careful not to blame but simply share and then try to say positive things and to love at the same time. It works really well.

By the way, even though Christian is the principal author here, I want the spouse with mental health conditions to know how much I feel for you. It's not easy always feeling like the bad guy—the one who is always causing pain for their spouse. That's a burden neither your spouse nor anyone else can understand. On top of everything else that was happening, I had to bear that. Don't give up.

## Get to the Root of Emotional Triggers: AGRUP

Here's a practical technique that will help you understand your feelings and gain insight into what triggers your spouse's feelings. Mastering this technique can help prevent emotional escalation—for your spouse and you.

In the early-to-middle years of our marriage, I often tried to sit down with Helen and calmly talk through important matters. But how was I to know that asking her to talk about our mutual needs in a respectful and calm way would lead to an instant blowup where she said I was trying to set her up for divorce? What was the chain of thought that led to her instant anger and drawing that kind of conclusion? I was baffled, angry, and left shaking my head.

It always happened lightning fast. In later years, I was able to recognize when it was happening by observing her expressions. In an instant, irrepressible anger would fill her eyes and further conversation became futile.

The book *Key Core Beliefs* provides brilliant insight into understanding human emotions. Authors Otis, Williams, and Messina explain it like this: *"Because [negative feelings] occur so quickly, it is crucial to emphasize that we are almost never conscious of our underlying primary feelings."*[4]

In other words, there are "triggering" *primary* feelings that fire off so fast we're not even aware of them. These feelings are the real troublemakers.

Get ready for an astonishing, game-changing fact.

The key, it turns out, is to identify these primary feelings, which precede becoming angry, sad, or anxious. Research shows this applies to *all* human beings, whether mentally healthy or ill. The primary feelings that trigger anger, sadness, or anxiety form the acronym AGRUP.

- A – Accused
- G – Guilty
- R – Rejected
- U – Unlovable
- P – Powerless

Let's do a quick exercise to illustrate how game-changing an awareness of the AGRUP feelings can be for your relationship.

Think back to a recent conflict with your spouse where *you* were emotionally upset. Try to recall the conversation from the very beginning and when you started to feel angry, sad, or anxious.

Take your time.

. . .

This is important.

. . .

Don't continue reading until you recall your feelings.

. . .

Do you feel those feelings? Let yourself feel them again.

. . .

Now, let's consider the AGRUP feelings one at a time.

- Was there anything your spouse said or did that made you feel **accused**, directly or indirectly (or even self-accused)?
- Was there anything that triggered you to feel **guilty**?
- Did you feel **rejected**?
- Did you feel **unloved** or unlovable?
- Did you feel **powerless**?

Identify these feelings one at a time, if they were there.

Did you recognize one or more?

Can you see why the AGRUP feelings are considered "primary"? Research shows that one or more of these *always* precede anger, sadness, or anxiety.

Very likely, you did recall one or more of the AGRUP feelings prior to getting angry, sad, or anxious that day. Just now—that scintillating insight probably impelled you to do a series of jubilant cartwheels, flips, and somersaults all through your neighborhood and you are back home in your seat and reading again. Phew!

Okay, perhaps you're not that exuberant.

Yet.

Now, let's consider what your *spouse* likely felt during that same conflict. Go through the AGRUP feelings again.

- Was there anything said or done that may have triggered him or her to feel **accused**, directly or indirectly or even self-accused?
- Was there anything that may have triggered feeling **guilty**?
- How about **rejected**?
- **Unloved** or **unlovable**?
- **Powerless**?

Can you see how these underlying feelings could cause a major bout of anger, sadness, or anxiety in your spouse? Are you looking at that incident a bit differently now? Is the fog of feelings and emotional reactions clearing just a bit?

Knowing that all humans are triggered by AGRUP feelings is one of the most important breakthroughs in understanding and preventing emotional flare-ups. We recommend you read *Key Core Beliefs* for more detail and practical activities to do with or without your spouse.

Understanding these reactions within yourself will help you monitor and feel your own feelings.

> 💡 It's easier to deal with a lightning-fast snake when you know exactly what it looks like, where it's hiding, and how it acts.

AGRUP feelings are like snakes hidden within us and others.

Instead of being confused by your spouse's jumble of intense emotions, you can become more sensitive to how your words, tone, and facial expressions may trigger your spouse to feel accused, guilty, rejected, unloved, or powerless—and vice versa.

Ideally, you can introduce your spouse to the concept of AGRUP feelings, and you can both experience an enlightenment.

## A Word about Culture and Speaking Openly

Perhaps it's not okay to talk about mental health issues and difficult feelings where you live and worship. Or so it seems. You may worry that people will fear or blame you if you mention that you or a family member are dealing with mental health or emotional issues.

Thankfully, the stigmas surrounding these issues have decreased in recent years. My wife and I made a decision years ago to speak openly about our conditions not as a badge of courage but rather as an acknowledgment that these conditions exist and are no more embarrassing than discussing a broken arm or a diagnosis of diabetes. This stuff happens, it's real, and we all need support and guidance to get through it. And it feels fantastic when you can be more open.

Being prudently and appropriately open about your experiences is good for others and therapeutic for you. It says, in effect, "I'm okay. My feelings are okay. And I may be able to help you."

I regularly speak to church congregations, and I often feel impressed to share relevant and encouraging bits of our story and mental health conditions as part of my message. I am never graphic or demeaning, nor do I glorify what we have been through. Without exception, people come up to me afterward and thank me for speaking candidly about this topic, or they ask me for additional information. There is a hunger for being open about these conditions because these issues are pervasive, especially in modern societies.

Your courage to share can encourage others to be more open and get help. This assumes you have your spouse's consent, which, of course, may be a huge decision that can take months or even years to reach. I have that consent to share our story, but even so, I focus mostly on my issues and recovery.

# Hope and Help

## Scriptures to Ponder

> *What time I am afraid, I will trust in thee. In God I will*
> *praise his word, in God I have put my trust; I will not*
> *fear what flesh can do unto me. (Psalm 56:3-4)*

> *Humble yourselves therefore under the mighty hand of God,*
> *that he may exalt you in due time: Casting all your care*
> *upon him; for he careth for you. (1 Peter 5:6-7)*

> *Happy is the man that findeth wisdom, and the man that getteth*
> *understanding. For the merchandise of it is better than the merchandise*
> *of silver, and the gain thereof than fine gold. (Proverbs 3:13-14)*

## What You Can Do Today

- Name a feeling as you feel it rising within you. Notice it, acknowledge it, accept it, and then let it flow right out of you. Do this as you interact with your spouse, family members, friends, coworkers, or anyone at all.
- To help you recognize the AGRUP emotions in yourself and stop triggering them in your spouse (which is not always possible), do the following exercise recommended by Otis, Williams, and Messina:
  - Mentally revisit a past conflict or painful experience in your life, from childhood through today, with any other person.

> □    Try to recall which of the AGRUP feelings you felt that
> caused the pain. You will be astonished at how well you may
> remember specific feelings from long ago.

Do this exercise at least once every day. The more you do it, the
quicker it will go and the more it will become ingrained in your
emotional intelligence and repertoire.

## Spiritual Blessings for You

Look forward to these wonderful blessings of patiently persevering
with your spouse or loved one in partnership with God.

- Greater emotional intelligence, meaning the ability to perceive your
  own and others' emotional states and respond appropriately[5]
- More precise, intentional use of words, including avoiding words
  that inflame and trigger negative responses
- Greater empathy when communicating with those who are
  emotionally erratic and make you uncomfortable
- Greater love and tolerance for those who are different than you, in
  your workplace, community, and the world generally

## Chapter 3
# I'm Starting to Doubt Myself and My Faith

In the previous chapter we considered the impact of your spouse's emotions on your emotions. Now, let's take a closer look at the other flavors of disruption you have likely experienced: nonsensical, irrational perceptions, ideas, and words, often combined with extreme or erratic emotions.

How do you think any rational person would be affected if someone they loved exhibited one or more of these behaviors?

- Unreasonable statements or accusations
- Relentless repetition of thoughts or accusations
- Intensely self-centered thinking and actions
- Little or no empathy for others' feelings and needs
- Inability to focus, listen, or pay attention
- Impulsive, irresponsible behaviors, spending sprees, etc.
- "Wearing a mask" of normalcy outside the home
- Eating binges and dietary fixations
- Compulsive, repetitive behaviors and obsessions
- Drug, alcohol, pornography, or other addictions

These behaviors wreak havoc on our homes. Some days, the spouses we love act like the beautiful people we fell in love with. Other days, even hour to hour, they hurt and bewilder us.

How do we make sense of it all? As humans and spouses, we crave consistency and reliability. Yet most of us can relate to this statement written about someone with borderline personality disorder (BPD).

> *Trying to define the BPD is like staring into a lava*
> *lamp: what you see is constantly changing.*[1]

The impact of our spouse's irrational conduct and endless inconsistency is often twofold:

1. We begin to doubt our own perceptions, opinions, desires, and beliefs.
2. If faith was ever an important part of our life, we may doubt that God is there anymore. Or, worse yet, we feel "played" and betrayed by God. Perhaps God played a nasty trick, yanking the rug out from under our feet with an evil smirk, watching us fall helpless onto our backs and ignoring our cries for help.

Your experiences with your spouse constitute God's advanced training for you in the topics of "What is reality?" and "What is faith?"

Your first objective is to get clear about what is real.

## The Defective Helmet Analogy

Imagine for a moment that your spouse has a helmet covering their whole head. It has eyeglasses, earpieces, and a mouthpiece, kind of like an old-fashioned diver's helmet. Imagine each of those pieces is not functioning properly. What your spouse sees isn't accurate. What they hear isn't accurate. And often, what comes out of their mouth is not coming from the heart of who they *really* are—the person you truly know and love.

Here's a quote that applies in some ways to all mental conditions. It was written by a person with BPD:

> *Borderlines and non-borderlines live in two different worlds*
> *that coexist in the same space but not always in the same time.*
> *Comprehending the "real" world, for me, is as formidable as the*
> *task of understanding the borderline world is for you.*[2]

That's astonishing, isn't it? Two different worlds? As hard as it is for the mentally ill person to understand our "real world," it's that hard for us to understand their world. That's a sobering thought.

Whether your spouse has PTSD (post-traumatic stress disorder) from military service, OCD (obsessive-compulsive disorder), clinical depression, adult ADHD (attention deficit hyperactivity disorder), or any other disorder, you and your spouse see, hear, and perceive many things differently.

Apart from my spouse's conditions, you may recall I was diagnosed with bipolar disorder 2, which makes me frequently depressed if untreated. Then, on top of that came the PTSD from the stresses of our challenging marriage. For years, I felt like I was in a slimy emotional pit I simply couldn't climb out of. But the effects went far beyond emotional depression.

I watched other people who seemed to have amazing energy and mental acuity. It was like their brain had a computer processor ten times faster than mine and they were just wired better.

*How do they laugh so heartily, what makes their eyes sparkle, and how do they talk with such vigor and joy?* I wondered. *How can they deal with great stresses and complicated situations so quickly and easily when I get bogged down, depressed, and lack confidence all the time?* I tried so hard to be positive and have energy, but I sensed people could tell I wasn't all there. And I could tell I lacked something fundamental.

My interpretations of what I heard and felt were filtered through my mental illness. My brain chemistry was affecting how I perceived the world and myself. It was affecting what I said and how I said it.

My depressive behaviors were torture for my wife, who needed me to be consistent, strong, and positive. It didn't matter that her issues aggravated my issues. The fact is that I had an illness and my behavior was affecting her happiness and satisfaction in our marriage, as well as the other way around.

## How to Set Your Feet on Solid Ground

Let's take a look at three actions you can take to stop second-guessing your perceptions and ground yourself in what is real.

Photo by Benjamin Lambert

1.  Learn about your spouse's condition.
2.  Don't engage in unproductive conversation.
3.  Say simple, positive, hopeful things.

### Action One: Learn about Your Spouse's Condition

There is something enormously stress-relieving when you understand what is really going on with your spouse. This miracle of understanding clears the fog and helps you confidently stand on ground you know is real.

For the first ten years of our marriage, I hadn't "cracked the code" to understanding my wife's condition. I can't begin to describe the relief I felt when I found a book called *Stop Walking on Eggshells* and I read this brief story:

> *Being married to [my spouse] is heaven one minute, hell the next. My wife's moods change by the second. I'm walking on eggshells trying to please her and avoid a fight for speaking too soon, too quickly, in the wrong tone, or with the wrong facial motions.*
>
> *Even when I do exactly as she asks, she gets mad at me. One day she ordered me to take the kids somewhere because she wanted some time alone. But as we were leaving, she threw the keys at my head and accused me of hating her so much I couldn't stand to be in the house with her.*
>
> *When the kids and I got back from the movie she acted like nothing had happened. She wondered why I was still upset and told me that I have problems letting go of my anger.[3]*

I could relate to every detail. It was so similar to what I had experienced for *years*! The book was full of stories and perfectly described my wife's disorder. My confidence about what was real and reasonable began to grow. Had I been the one who was unreasonable in so many of our conflicts, as she asserted? Did I have an anger problem, as she so often accused, because I was still upset and fearful after yet another mind-bending episode?

No! *Exhale* No.

The first step for a victim of emotional abuse and mental chaos to planting their feet on solid ground is to understand the nature of their loved one's condition. Decipher the code.

> 💡 Once I understood the nature of my spouse's condition and how it all worked, I felt like a new man. I had hope and clarity.

Fortunately, you don't have to figure it out yourself.

If you haven't already, save yourself years of self-doubt and confusion by getting heads-down busy researching your spouse's condition. Even if they haven't been diagnosed, you can begin reading based on what you are observing. If it's not a mental illness you suspect but an addiction, the same applies. You will gain insights into the behavior patterns, underlying thought patterns, and coping skills needed for you and for them. And, of course, do your best to get a medical diagnosis or addiction treatment, assuming your spouse will cooperate.

## Action Two: Don't Engage in Unproductive Conversation

Try to vividly imagine this scenario: you are trying to communicate with a deep-sea diver who is wearing a helmet that has eyepieces with red tint and earpieces that play sounds of swirling sharks and creepy background music.

This diver is convinced his experience is real.

The diver repeatedly explains that there's blood in the water. There are awful sounds of sharks brushing past him. Yet for an hour, you attempt to correct him about anything he says that isn't accurate. He gets angrier and counters everything you say. You explain that his helmet must have a problem, but then he accuses you of being unsupportive, unhelpful, inconsiderate, and not grounded in the facts. "You are out of touch," he says.

Clearly, you are wasting your time and potentially confusing yourself.

Typically, a mentally ill or addicted person in denial will become more and more annoyed. They will try to force you to see things *their* way. They may be extremely articulate and persuasive and actually start shifting your thinking.

> ꙮ Get off the merry-go-round. Do not participate in unproductive conversation. Create a boundary that says, "I have the right to stop engaging in a conversation that has become harmful."

This doesn't mean you have to stop talking altogether, but it might. Consider this advice from the coauthor of a book on marriage and mental illness:

> *Trying to have a rational, meaningful discussion when a [mentally ill] person is in a psychotic state is nearly impossible. . . . The best thing I ever learned was that I could not fix [my spouse]—all I could do was control and repair myself. I realized I couldn't go up and down with his highs and lows. It was emotionally impossible and would drive me crazy trying to do it.*[4]

We cannot pry the helmet off our spouse's head. Nor is that our role. Helping our spouses learn to understand their condition is the role of a mental health or addiction recovery professional. We can acknowledge and thank our spouses for positive behaviors. We can appropriately express our feelings and communicate boundaries. But we cannot be the primary healer, rescuer, and teacher.

Resist the temptation to show how right you are, thinking that you will enlighten your spouse. In small doses, perhaps, and when the Holy Spirit gently prompts you, yes. But too often we're just trying to make ourselves feel better by "helping" our spouse. Ponder this biblical advice:

> *A fool takes no pleasure in understanding, but only in expressing his opinion. (Proverbs 18:2, ESV)*

> *A fool uttereth all his mind: but a wise man keepeth it in till afterwards. (Proverbs 29:11)*

*Whoso keepeth his mouth and his tongue keepeth
his soul from troubles. (Proverbs 21:23)*

That last scripture is profound. How many times I desperately tried to reel the words back into my mouth because the consequences and backlash of my lectures or well-meaning explanations were so brutal. Too often, my attempts to counter, teach, correct, and enlighten my spouse got me into trouble.

In today's language, it's worth asking,

*"Would you rather be right or be married?"*

*—Anonymous*

## Helen's Perspective

[How she would have felt years ago]: My husband hates me. All I hear when he lectures me is, "You're ugly. You're fat. He hates you. You're no good for him." I mean, I really hear those things in my head and don't even hear what he is saying. I just stare and think how much I shouldn't live anymore because nobody loves me. Why can't anybody love me? I'm a nice person. I try to be nice to people. Why do they have to treat me like this?

[Fast-forward twenty-seven years]: Sometimes I feel the same as above, although now I usually know he loves me. I've received better medications that really, really help and almost make the voices go away. But Christian is also a lot smarter about how he talks to me. If he were to start being mean again, I would get really depressed. Those voices are never too far away.

My dialectical behavior therapy (DBT) changed our lives, too, I have to say. I was in a full-time treatment program for three months. For the first time, I understood that how I was responding to things was not helpful for either of us. I saw other program participants who were not well, and they thought they saw things that weren't even there—I mean really hallucinating, like yelling for us to run because the building was on fire. I saw that it's possible to be seriously out of touch with what is real. That was eye-opening and really scary.

But for me, the biggest problem has always been my feelings getting out of control, and they taught me tricks for managing that. It changed my life, our life. Thank you, Heavenly Father, for saving our marriage because of the good people who taught me these things.

## Action Three: Say Simple, Positive, Hopeful Things

Consider this approach for halting or redirecting unproductive conversations: when your spouse is having trouble communicating effectively, instead of countering their actions and thoughts, find ways to slow things down and say, "I love you."

Later in our life, when my wife was exhausted from arguing, she came to understand the risks of continual arguing. And I learned how to diffuse situations by simply hugging her and saying things like:

"I love you."

"Things will get better."

"I know it hurts and it's hard right now."

"I'm sorry you're hurting."

"I love you."

"Today was a tough day."

"I love you."

"I know this is hard to deal with."

"I love you, and I know God loves both of us."

"God is here, and He will never leave us."

"I love you."

Obviously, saying such things cannot be mechanical or insincere. It takes the power of God within you to lift you above the crisis and strengthen your heart. God can help you focus on the positive feelings you have for your spouse and say tender things even amid unkind words and accusations. My spouse didn't magically stop fighting when I said such things, but it prevented further escalation and gradually calmed things down.

Sometimes the issues that cause a fight are important and pressing, like the demands of a job, the kids' needs, commitments to attend an event, etc. The desire to keep talking about the issue to resolve it can feel intense and necessary. But if the conversation isn't working, it is harmful, and it's best to change course. Consider this wise counsel from Thomas S. Monson:

> 💡 "Never let a problem to be solved become more important than a person to be loved."[5]

What your spouse often needs most is language and behavior that builds, compliments, and soothes.

On the other hand, our patient, kind words simply may not help. When a spouse is having a severe episode, they may reject your attempts to love them. They may want to keep arguing. In such cases, you must breathe deep and enforce your boundaries.

Chapter 8, "My Spouse Is Walking All Over Me" is dedicated to this important topic, but here's a sneak peek about what constitutes boundaries in a relationship:

> *Boundaries are guidelines, rules, or limits a person creates to identify reasonable, safe, and permissible ways for other people to behave towards them and how they will respond when someone passes those limits.*[6]

When your limits are repeatedly passed, you risk losing your sense of self and your reality begins to be compromised. For many spouses of the mentally ill, allowing their boundaries to be grievously and repeatedly crossed is a key reason they feel so confused and awful. Feel free to jump to chapter 8 if you sense this is an important topic for you.

## My Faith Is on the Ropes!

Photo by PA Photos
(Ricky Burns v.
Terrance Crawford, 2014)

The most important grounding in reality we need is our faith in God and the gospel of Jesus Christ.

But is your faith ever challenged? Are you ever like this boxer?

A boxer is said to be "on the ropes" when he has backed up as far as he can and continues to be pummeled mercilessly by his opponent.

Our faith in God can also be pummeled by repeated disappointments, unfair accusations, emotional drain, evaporating dreams, and constant confusion. A spouse who is trying to maintain faith may start wondering:

- "Why don't I feel God helping me when I need Him most?"
- "I prayed about this marriage and felt it was right."
- "Why am I not experiencing God's blessings? I've been so faithful to His commandments!"
- "I think my faith has been a waste."

Personally, I have to confess I never experienced a sense of betrayal or doubt where God was concerned. I had already been through a faith crisis before we were married. My experience emerging from that crisis was so positive, vivid, and powerful that I never seriously doubted the divinity of Jesus Christ or the truthfulness of the scriptures again.[7]

I did, however, have doubts about specific doctrines and wondered if I was being punished. I also questioned if I was hearing God's answers correctly, and I struggled to trust those answers.

## How We Respond to Hard Times

When a believer faces hard times, it's tempting to move a bit toward the left on this continuum of possible responses.

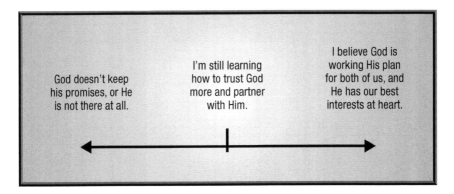

This book is designed to help you move to the right—to deepen your faith and see how God's purposes for you are being fulfilled through your challenging relationship. Ideally, you feel yourself more solidly moving from the center to the far right, where you accept God's plan for your life and develop spiritual skills that help you thrive.

If you feel yourself moving to the left, give some careful thought to these faith-restoring recommendations inspired by author and pastor Jim Stout, who also suffers from mental illness:[8]

1. **Accept the wisdom of the old question: "If I feel like God is far away, who moved?"** We are the ones who allow our hardships to move us away from God. God didn't simply leave us. We can correct this through a submissive spirit, regular prayer, and immersing ourselves in scripture again. God may withdraw His Spirit to a degree, but He never truly leaves us. He is ever near and waiting.

2. **Pray what you feel in raw, bluntly honest terms, if necessary.** Don't just pray "pretty things" you think you're supposed to pray. Have it out with God. Go where nobody can hear you and tell Him out loud everything you ever wanted to say to His face. Tell Him what you're feeling, frankly and bluntly, with all your emotional hurt pouring out like blood. Then, in the days that follow, keep silently talking, listening, and feeling.

3. **Reflect on the many past heroes** who endured affliction and crises of faith, like Job, David, Paul, and, more recently, Martin Luther, who wrote: *"I was close to the gates of death and hell. I trembled in all my members. Christ was wholly lost. I was shaken by depression. . . . I disputed much with God with great impatience."*[9]

4. **Come to terms with your losses and allow yourself to grieve over them.** Consider that God's pruning of the things you hoped for may be preparing you to bear His fruit in more abundance but in a different way. *"Every branch that does bear fruit he prunes so that it will be even more fruitful."* See John 15:2.

5. **Be constructively honest and open with others about your sagging faith.** Abandon worries about what people think of you (or the image you hoped people would have of you) and get real about your truest feelings. Seek others' perspectives. There is relief in heart-to-heart conversation. You will find your credibility is even greater as you are willing to be vulnerable and work through it. And know, too, that God respects and answers honest, open questions. (See Jeremiah 33:3 and James 1:5.)

6. **In the end, believe God wants to help you.** Eventually, make the conscious decision to believe that God truly is good. At some point, you have to make up your mind and just commit. Walk over the line of doubt and anger. Step over it. Stay there. Keep walking with the daily thought, *I believe in Jesus Christ. I believe He is good. I believe the Father loves me and knows what is best. I believe His promises are fulfilled but I may not understand how long and hard the road may be before I see their fulfillment. I believe Jesus is ready and eager to fill me with His gifts. I choose to bow before Him in worship and humbly accept His gifts.* (If desired, jump to chapter 12: "Joyful After All" and read the section, "Surrender: It's Not a Dirty Word" for a vivid metaphor of how to make this choice.)

# Hope and Help

## Scriptures to Ponder

*Call unto me, and I will answer thee, and show thee great and mighty things, which thou knowest not. (Jeremiah 33:3)*

*He that cometh to God must believe that he is, and that he is a rewarder of them that diligently seek him. (Hebrews 11:6)*

*Before I was afflicted I went astray: but now have I kept thy word. (Psalm 119:67)*

## What You Can Do Today

- Research your spouse's mental health condition or addiction. Search online support groups or join live discussions with others so you can share your stories and receive validation.
- Express your feelings in a letter to your spouse's *disorder*, not your spouse. If your spouse has an OCD diagnosis, write what you would like to say to the OCD disorder if it were a person standing in front of you. Let it rip. Rail away. Share your feelings and get them on paper. This will help you separate the illness or condition

from your spouse. The imposter/monster is not your spouse, and this activity can relieve boatloads of stress while addressing your feelings to the correct party.[10]

- If a tense communication situation comes up today:

    1. Don't engage in unproductive conversation.
    2. Say simple, positive, hopeful things.
    3. Look to the Holy Spirit to prompt you on how to communicate. Stop relying on your own thinking and have a prayer in your heart, such as, "Dear Father, guide my thoughts and words to be wise."

- If your faith is sagging, work through the action steps recommended earlier in the "My Faith Is on the Ropes!" section.

## Spiritual Blessings for You

Look forward to the wonderful blessings of patiently persevering with your spouse or loved one in partnership with God:

- More steadfastness and commitment to follow God first
- Greater ability to rise above adversity—including personal attacks—and stay positive and constructive
- Greater wisdom to communicate well in tough situations, which benefits you inside and outside the home
- More compassion for human weaknesses and foibles

## Chapter 4

# Can I Survive This?

Anyone who has been married to someone with a serious emotional or mental illness or addiction is at some point going to ask themselves, "Can I survive this?"

The pain and confusion get so intense that our self-preservation instinct kicks in. We wrestle with a million questions, but we keep coming back to this fundamental dilemma:

- Should I stay in this relationship?
- Should I leave for my survival?

Such churning questions can torment us for months and even years.

If this sounds familiar, you might breathe a little easier knowing you are not the only one who thinks like that. It's an understandable, natural reaction. It's survival.

## Get God's Answer

This chapter is placed near the beginning of this book for a reason. You can put the deliberation to rest. Here's how:

> 💡 The best way to survive and feel happier is to make sure you're committed, confident, and in it for the long haul. You can get that kind of confidence from God.

You need God's seal of approval.

You need God's answer in your heart to sustain you.

31

Acknowledging that there may be situations in which it is best to part ways, we also believe that walking out on a marriage in a huff or even after years of careful thinking—but without really knowing that God sanctions your decision to separate—is unwise. This decision is too important to rely on limited human emotion or perspective. God will provide an answer if you seek it through sincere prayer.

When you feel that sweet confirmation to stay married (or remind yourself and let your heart feel it again), there's a blessed change of heart that releases you from the energy-sucking, mental ping-pong of wondering whether to stay or leave the relationship. The more *meaning* you feel in your choice, the more power you will have to sustain you through difficult times. Then you can focus on this more constructive question: "What can we do with the help of God to fulfill the plan He has for us as a family?"

## The Holy Spirit versus Human Opinion

The Holy Spirit is the member of the Godhead who testifies, comforts, teaches, and provides guidance through the "still, small voice," as God described it to the prophet Elijah (1 Kings 19:11–13). In my experience, no feeling or understanding has ever touched me so deeply as the Holy Spirit enlightening me or testifying that something is true.

For example, how did Simon Peter, the ancient apostle, know Jesus Christ wasn't just a weirdo with interesting ideas and an inflated ego? Peter knew it because God revealed it to him long before He ever saw Christ come back from the dead. I like this simplified translation of a dialogue between Jesus and Peter:

> [Jesus] asked them, "But who do you say I am?"
>
> Simon Peter answered, "You are the Messiah, the Son of the living God."
>
> Jesus replied, "You are blessed, Simon . . . because my Father in heaven has revealed this to you. You did not learn this from any human being." (Matthew 16:15-17, NLT)

Human beings cannot answer the question "Should I stay or should I leave my spouse?"

- Not your parents
- Not your well-meaning siblings and friends
- Not the advice or stories on social media
- Not this book

Your loved ones have probably filled your head with well-meaning advice. Mine did.

## My Well-Meaning Father

My spouse and I lived in physically separate places for a few months or more on four different occasions throughout our first fifteen years of marriage. I initiated each of these separations. Each one ended up being beneficial.

However, after one of the longest periods—which initially was headed for divorce—I told my parents I intended to get back together with Helen.

Not long after, I got a letter from my father in which he felt obligated to warn me and chastise me in love for making the wrong decision. He had never written such a letter to me. While I was reading it, I felt in my heart that this advice was not in line with the answer God had put into my heart, so I respectfully put it aside.

This type of thing happened over and over with many different people. All the while, I had to remember what God had told me. His answer wasn't just in my head. It was deep, deep in my heart, and I knew I had God's support in moving forward with what He had spoken to my heart: "Your marriage to Helen is right in my eyes. It is right for both of you. Much good will come out of these ordeals for you and both of your families."

## Why We Need Powerful Help from God

Here's an example of why I needed such a deep and certain confirmation from God.

One of the things I most dreaded in our marriage was when Helen was on an out-of-control roller coaster. After a while, I would have enough of an argument and try to stop the conversation. But she would get even angrier and yell, "You got me started! You're not going to stop talking to me now!"

In the early years of our marriage, she could go on for hours. It was maddening. We had been to a psychologist who advised us to come up with a signal where we would agree to leave the other person alone because one or the other felt violated. Our signal was supposed to be the phrase "Red Flag."

The first time I said, "Red Flag," Helen paused just long enough to recall why I might have said those words and then went right on where she left off. It had absolutely no effect.

Saying "Calm down" was like giving her dynamite. Not an option. I recall going to another room in the house and locking the door, hoping I might be safe. She followed me. She banged on the door. She sat outside the door. She cried. She continued yelling and trying to convince me of whatever I needed convincing of.

I recall incredulously thinking, *How long can she go on like this*? I experienced close to an hour or more of mounting horror at what was happening, but before long, I began to question the appropriateness of "hiding," and so I gave up and came out.

Until she truly exhausted herself from the arguing and yelling, she would keep going. And it was my responsibility, in her mind, to stay with her since I had "started it"—which could have been anything from looking at her wrong, to an irritating remark, to doing something accidentally, or saying something truly stupid and hurtful.

The good news is that much later in life, Helen learned that arguing in such a way harmed us, and she did this less and less often to where it *never* happens anywhere near this extent today. Do we still have disagreements? Yes. But not like that.

But how long can a person survive such episodes without serious help and comfort from God? I needed it, and I got it.

## Helen's Perspective

[How she would have felt years ago]: I don't want my husband reading anything about my mental health. I know he wants to leave me anyway because I'm terrible for him. Anything he reads will just prove he should leave. He doesn't need more proof that I'm a terrible person.

We try hard to be close to God, but I don't want him to pray about our marriage. God knows what I'm like. I'm no good for him. Why even ask the question?

I don't think it's right that Christian should be thinking about leaving me. I told him I had problems when we met. I need his help, and I don't want to feel like he is ready to leave me every time I make a mistake. I hate that. It's not right. We are a family, and I need him. He knows that.

If I find out he is planning to leave me, I will seriously hurt myself! I can't live with that. I can't stand the thought of being alone and having another person say I'm not good enough. Oh, God, why would you tell him to leave me?

[Fast-forward twenty-seven years]: Christian separated from me four times. It helped every time, and things got better. I hated it, but it did help. I still struggle with the fear that I will never be good enough, but my understanding that we both have feelings and needs has grown. I can have empathy for his need to have stability. I didn't know it, but empathy was almost impossible for me before. And I used to be afraid God wouldn't support him staying with me, even though we both had prayed before our marriage and felt that it was right.

## How to Get Answers to Prayer

Perhaps it will help to review the basics of prayer. If you're confident in your ability to receive answers to prayer, feel free to skip this section.

1. **Learn to recognize answers from God.** If you are not familiar with getting answers to prayer, this could be a months-long process for you. You can't force it. Learning to really communicate with God is likely one of the things He wants you to learn from this challenging experience with your spouse. Talk to your spiritual leaders/advisors about how to pray. Start by praying about smaller, short-term decisions. Study scriptures and stories about prayer. Talk to friends about how they get answers. You have to figure this out sooner or later. It is critical to your spiritual life and survival in this relationship.

2. **Be Specific.** Praying something like the following probably won't help much: "Dear God, help me to know if I should stay with my spouse. Amen." Instead, share the facts with God in detail. Talk to

Him like a Father you know is perfect. Talk about your desires for the future, your shattered dreams, your fears. Talk about whatever you need to talk about to get everything related to your marriage out in the open.

Here's an example: "Heavenly Father, I love you so much and praise you for the gift of life. My life is hard, and I really hate (such and such), but I know I can grow through this. I'm grateful for (such and such good thing that happened today). I'm even trying to be grateful for (such and such rotten situation). But I'm so worn out because of (such and such). I felt like doing (such and such), but I didn't. I don't know what to do tomorrow. For now, I think I should do (such and such). Protect me if this is wrong. Redirect my thoughts. Go before my face. Please strengthen me as I face (such and such specific situation). Dear Father, I love you. I want to feel your love more, but it's so hard when (such and such) happens. Most of all, please help me know if I should stay in this marriage. For all of (such and such reasons), I feel I should (or should not), but you know the beginning from the end. In Jesus's name, amen."

3. **Recognize that an answer from God doesn't typically answer everything.** I sought and received an answer to prayer and fasting even before I married my wife. And given the severity of what I experienced after we married, I sought confirmation often and received it often. I knew the marriage was right—even though I had a bazillion-trillion unanswered questions. But that's okay. The main question was answered, and that gave me the power, confidence, and peace (on most days) to live, learn, and grow. Moving ahead in life with a partial, imperfect understanding is built into the plan of our earthly experience—and just because we have mentally and emotionally challenged family members doesn't give us a pass on the requirement to live by faith with partial information, trusting in the Lord. (See 1 Corinthians 13:12)

4. **Fast.** To "fast" means to go without food. A common timeframe for fasting is about twenty-four hours. Fasting is mentioned extensively in both the Old and New Testaments. Jesus did it for forty days. (Don't try this at home!) Jesus fasted because it is

beneficial and enhances communication with God. Don't overlook fasting when you need a clear answer to an important question. God will respect your sacrifice, and you will be more sensitive to His Spirit if you do it. I always feel more confident and clear about my answers to prayer when I'm fasting.

## Abuse and Illegal Activity

Some relationships should end. Although this book takes the position that most marriages can survive with God's help, some are dangerous. Know with 100 percent certainty that God does not expect you to submit to abuse. Patiently persevere at times, yes.

Here are some strong indicators that your relationship may *not* be right for you and that you may need to end it or at least take measures to temporarily make life safer for you. You've probably thought about these already, but it helps to specifically call them out and factor them into your prayers.

### Abuse

Abuse comes in many forms, as summarized below. You need to be on the lookout for these in order to protect yourself.

| Type of Abuse | What It Looks Like |
|---|---|
| Verbal/Emotional/ Psychological Abuse | Intimidation, manipulation, refusal to ever be pleased, blaming, shaming, name-calling, insults, sarcasm, constant yelling despite being asked to stop, threatening, and more. See the endnote for far more detailed descriptions and recommendations for how to respond.[1] |
| Physical Abuse | Hitting, beating, slapping, strangling, scratching, pinning down, jerking around, etc. |
| Sexual Abuse | Your spouse forces or attempts to force unwanted sexual activities on you or withholds it and rations it to manipulate or punish you. |

| Type of Abuse | What It Looks Like |
|---|---|
| Financial/ Economic | Your spouse keeps you "under control" by restricting your access to money, mail, other people, or by creating financial conditions that make it feel impossible to get out of the relationship. |

## Extreme Risk/Illegal Activities

Sexual and physical abuse are illegal by themselves. But the following behaviors can take the relationship to an even darker level.

| | |
|---|---|
| Addictions to Substances | Alcohol and street/prescription drug abuse by your spouse greatly intensify the chaos and danger of a relationship. |
| Crime | Drug dealing, shoplifting, white-collar theft, or any type of illegal schemes detract from the Spirit of God in your relationship and create a host of additional risk factors for you and your family. |
| Weapons | Spouses with mental conditions, including "departure from reality," such as paranoid schizophrenia, can do dangerous things out of fear. They may be convinced that extreme actions, including stockpiling and carrying weapons, are necessary to protect themselves. Or they may have hate ideologies and fantasies of destruction. |

Any of these abusive or illegal behaviors should factor heavily into your decision.

Think about it. How can you move forward on a journey to strengthen your marriage where Satan has free reign through such diabolical behaviors in your home? I believe that God does not expect you to endure it. It will confuse and harm you if you try to persevere and apply the recommendations in this book while being horribly abused and watching your children continually placed in danger.

If you are weighing the impact of a separation on your children, consider this statement from world-renown marriage researchers:

> One important message of [our] findings is that it is not wise
> to stay in a bad marriage for the sake of your children.[2]

We know children of divorced parents who tell us, "Life got better when our parents divorced. That was a living hell." To this day, they are grateful their parents divorced.

There are situations where it is best to separate. You'll recall that Helen and I separated several times, which was necessary for my healing and helped Helen "get better" by reducing her abusive behavior. I chose to rely on God as much as possible and hold out hope that further healing and improvement would come, which it did.

For your well-being and that of your family, you need to look your circumstance dead in the face with eyes wide open. You would likely agree that God is best qualified to answer to such a large, complex question as "Should I stay, or should I end the relationship?"

## Good News and Bad News: Deep Differences

As you pray, you may wish to consider this important insight from marriage research:

> Most marital arguments cannot be resolved. Couples spend year after
> year trying to change each other's mind—but it can't be done. . . . Instead
> they need to live with it by honoring and respecting each other.[3]

Seriously? Talk about bursting the bubble.

The good news is that these same researchers reported that nearly all couples who described themselves as happy had ongoing conflicts they couldn't resolve. (This does not include serious abuse and fundamental values conflicts, of course.) They just found better ways to deal with persistent differences than couples who ultimately divorced.

So, as you pray, if you sense you have deep, unresolvable differences in regard to personality, living preferences, and communication styles *on top of* your spouse's mental health or addiction issues, your relationship is not doomed. Some unresolvable conflicts are common in all marriages.

For example, take something as simple as the wife who says her husband drives too fast and she thinks he is selfish and inconsiderate for not listening to her wishes and respecting her fears. But the husband feels just as strongly that she should trust him because he has an impeccable driving record and is very safety minded.

This is most likely a conflict they will take to their graves (hopefully not in a car accident!). Helen and I learned that successful couples gradually improve how they compromise and find good-natured ways to get their point across, using kind-hearted, not snide remarks.

## An Example of Unresolvable Conflict

Helen loves to spend money on a whim, especially on clothes. To this day, the shirts on clothing racks call her name and wave her in. Budgeting became an unresolvable conflict a long time ago, but we found ways to deal with it.

Because of Helen's physical disability, I often helped with organizing her clothes. One year, some of her clothes were hanging up, but many lay piled on the floor. As I was sorting through the pile and hanging things, my head snapped back to a shirt I had just hung up.

*Wait a minute. This looks familiar!* I thought. Sure enough, the exact shirt was hanging up already, and both shirts still had the price tag on them!

Grrr.

Over time, Helen started treasure hunting for clothes at thrift shops. Goodwill and the Salvation Army loved the Bohlens as donators and buyers—especially when we pulled stunts like this:

One day after grocery shopping, Helen asked me to help her hang up her latest precious finds from her Goodwill expeditions that day (from multiple stores). As I pulled each shirt out of the bag with all the enthusiasm I could muster, my face fell as I held up a certain sweater for Helen to take a closer look.

"Uh, this one looks *very* familiar, don't you think?"

"Really?"

"Yeah. You just bought your own sweater back again, didn't you?"

We good-naturedly laughed as we remembered bagging up that same sweater and donating it just a few weeks earlier.

## The Marriage Triangle

This diagram, typically called the Marriage Triangle, illustrates how the closer you both come to God, the closer you get to each other. This triangle has been displayed and preached about for generations. Why? Because it speaks truth.

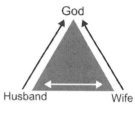

Even though there are biblically justifiable reasons to end a relationship, this book takes the view that marriage is a commitment—an all-in, covenant commitment of the deepest kind as described by Timothy and Kathy Keller:

> The covenant made between a husband and a wife is done "before God" and therefore with God as well as the spouse. To break faith with your spouse is to break faith with God at the same time.[4]

Notice the arrows in the triangle, which represent the covenant each spouse makes with each other but at the same time also with God. You and I are accountable to God for the diligent, devoted fulfillment of our covenant responsibilities before Him, unlike today's consumer mentality where we might switch to a new brand of bread or different restaurant when the former ones no longer suit us.[5]

💡 There is no better way to start improving your relationship with your spouse than to get closer to Jesus Christ. And there's no better place to develop Christlike attributes than in the marriage and family relationship.

I testify to the improvements that come into our lives when we seek God first and allow Him to change our natural tendency toward self-centeredness. Most of us are foolish and unskilled at the beginning of our marriages. What a difference it makes when we allow God to draw us higher.

Think back to the driving-too-fast example. Imagine how the tempering influence of the Holy Spirit could help that couple to:

- Speak with greater kindness and empathy
- Learn to say nothing
- Do it "the other person's way"—at least a little

You may be thinking, "But wait! I refuse to be a doormat! This isn't about me giving in all the time, is it?"

No, it is not, as you will see in the chapters that follow. There are ways to care for yourself while being more Christlike.

Yes, the Marriage Triangle is a worthy symbol of how to find happiness in your challenging marriage, even if your spouse isn't committed to a God-focused marriage at this time. Your commitment to God will still yield His increased gifts and wisdom for *you*, which will ultimately bless your union and your spouse.

## Can I Survive This?

So, back to the original question: *Can* you survive your marriage?

If your marriage is right and safe in God's eyes, you can.

Oh, how we wish you could see how terrified and hopeless we felt and how unskilled Helen and I were during those first torturous years together. If you find you're in a similar situation, it doesn't have to be that way forever. And here is some encouraging research to back it up:

> *Most striking of all, longitudinal studies demonstrate that two-thirds of . . . unhappy marriages out there will become happy within five years if people stay married and do not get divorced.*[6]

Clearly, there is hope. Keep reading.

# Hope and Help

## Scriptures to Ponder

> *Trust in the Lord with all thine heart; and lean not unto thine own understanding. (Proverbs 3:5)*

*I will instruct thee and teach thee in the way which thou*
*shalt go: I will guide thee with mine eye. (Psalm 32:8)*

*I can do all things through Christ which strengtheneth me. (Philippians 4:13)*

## What You Can Do Today

- Believe that God knows the end from the beginning and that it is wisest to trust Him over your own thoughts and fears or the advice you receive from others who mean well.
- Believe that God can help you do all things necessary for the ultimate success and happiness of your life and your family. If the relationship is right, you can survive and thrive.
- If you don't already have God's confirmation about your relationship, start seeking it today.

| Things I Love and Enjoy about [spouse] | Things that Challenge Me about [spouse] |
| --- | --- |
| | |

- To help your prayers be more focused and effective, grab a blank piece of paper and draw a T-chart like the one below.
  - This terrific exercise prompts balanced thinking. It reminds you there's more to your spouse than just his or her illness.

- What did you love and admire about your spouse when dating? What strengths do they have? In what ways have they helped you? What positive things would you miss if you were no longer married?
- When you're finished, don't just look at the number of items on each side. Some are far weightier than others.

## Spiritual Blessings for You

Look forward to these wonderful blessings of patiently persevering with your spouse or loved one in partnership with God.

- More faithfulness in praying often
- More confidence that you are getting answers to prayer
- Greater commitment to do your part to live a godly life regardless of how others behave
- Greater understanding of God's view of marriage

Chapter 5

# It's Not Fair

To put it bluntly, if you live with someone who has mental illness, your relationship with that person is simply unfair. It will never be fair.

Breathe deep.

Exhale.

Mourn if you have to.

Then get over it.

It's best to just accept that your relationship with your spouse is not going to be fair. "Fairness" may not be the most productive frame for assessing the value of your relationship anyway. It's a distressing thought, but it's best to look reality in the eye and find techniques that help you cope with it.

## Examples of Unfairness in Relationships

Perhaps some of these situations sound familiar to you:

- If your spouse tends to be depressive, you feel like you've always got to be chipper. You feel an excessive responsibility to maintain a good mood. You're usually the one who gets stuff done around the house. When you're feeling down, your spouse has no energy to lift you or work harder. That's unfair.
- Perhaps your spouse becomes financially irresponsible and goes on spending sprees, buying unnecessary things or feeding their addiction(s), so you have to hunker down all the time and watch your spending because the budget is stretched beyond limits all the time. You'd like to buy the occasional, tiny, nice-to-have item, but

whenever you do, it seems to trigger another free-for-all spending spree. That's unfair.

- If your spouse is easily irritated and their anger is unpredictable, you feel a burden to monitor your spouse's moods, your own thoughts, and your words to the extent you can hardly think for yourself anymore. You're constantly trying to avoid another round of contention. Then your spouse criticizes you for being uptight all the time. "What's wrong with you?" they flippantly ask, which hurts you. When you try to explain your feelings, it leads to another eruption, so you stay silent. That's unfair.

- What if your spouse has severe social anxiety and is reluctant to go outside or invite guests over? Your spouse used to love your energy and fearlessness around other people when you were dating, but now she seems to resent it because you "constantly" want to be around other people. You crave company, but your spouse craves *your* company alone and dislikes it when you go off to social events or even give church service to others because it's "just an excuse to go have fun." That's unfair.

- You're trying your best to draw near to God, but your troubled spouse has stopped looking to God even though you married with a clear understanding that you would have a God-centered home. How can you possibly make the Marriage Triangle work? That's unfair.

## What about "Normal" Marriages?

Even marriages without mental health issues struggle with perceived unfairness. This chapter does not focus on the typical sources of fairness conflict, such as who does more chores, who does which chores, who has more time or money available, who is better at remembering and scheduling important things, etc. Those are important.

However, when mental illness is involved, the unfairness typically strikes at even deeper and more confusing levels, requiring an even greater closeness to God to endure it wisely and gracefully.

This chapter is intended to help you see that unfairness is a common earthly condition and one of God's greatest pruning and shaping tools. Interestingly, it appears to be one of His favorite and most effective.

## An Example of Unfairness: The Cherry Turnover

My mother-in-law came to live with us at a critical time in our lives. Although she was skeptical that Helen was mentally ill during our early married years, that skepticism quickly faded once she experienced it herself. Here's a look back with a little tongue-in-cheek humor.

One day when Helen was in a bad mood, we took a drive to the closest town where there was a fast-food restaurant. This might seem like a simple, safe activity.

Not so.

Helen viewed employees at any fast-food restaurant with the greatest suspicion and contempt. They stood between her and what she wanted. Somehow, their incompetent brains and clumsy hands delivered a disproportionate number of goofed up orders to her, specifically, she was certain. A conspiracy!

We pulled up to the drive-through window. Helen wanted a cherry turnover. More than once, Helen's mother and I had heard Helen malign the employees for giving her the cursed *apple* turnover instead. This would result in a long tirade about how insensitive and uncaring these people were and how they'd ruined her day. If we dared speak a word on their behalf, we became the target.

After paying at the first window, we rolled forward to the second. A profound, fearful silence filled the car as we waited for the bag with the turnover to be handed through the drive-through window. The bag crinkled as she opened it.

"Apple!" she cried, and we hung our heads as a tirade ensued.

After several minutes of Helen venting her irritation, I softly suggested, "How about we turn around and get 'em to fix it?" This was initially rejected because Helen hated letting people correct their hurtful mistakes.

At length, hunger or weariness prevailed, and we headed back and explained the error. Once again, we trembled as the white bag was handed through the window.

Timidly, my mother-in-law muttered, "Dear God, let it be cherry."

We all erupted with laughter, including Helen.

The heavens smiled on us that day. It was cherry.

Over the months, my mother-in-law and I unfairly endured countless hours of tension as we tried to understand, avoid, and deal with Helen's overreactions to stressors of all shapes and sizes.

And isn't Helen's condition unfair to her? For years and years, she tried so hard to do what was right and to do better in so many ways. Time after time, I witnessed her make to-do lists and commitments on paper to accomplish a certain something. But the conviction and memory of the goal would evaporate in a couple of days.

Her ability to find peace in the Lord was sporadic as well. Her condition interfered with her thinking and emotions, creating unfair conditions for others that made her feel awful. That was unfair for her, too, because she bore the sadness and guilt of feeling like the bad person all the time.

## Before David Was King

As illustrated in scripture, unfairness comes in many varieties.

You may recall that many chapters in the first book of Samuel in the Old Testament describe King Saul's grossly unfair treatment of David (see 1 Samuel chapters 16–31). Even though David played lovely music for the king in his court, won battles for him, and refused to take revenge on him because the king was "the Lord's anointed," King Saul repeatedly threw spears at him and sent men to hunt him down and kill him. Seriously. Talk about unfair.

David truly loved the king and tried to help his cause. He must have been shocked and astonished by the king's unrelenting campaign to destroy him.

At one point, King Saul was sleeping near David's camp and became an easy target for David's revenge. David's men encouraged him to kill Saul while he had the chance. But consider David's wise answer:

*The Lord shall smite him; or his day shall come to die;*
*or he shall descend into battle and perish.*

*The Lord forbid that I should stretch forth mine hand against the Lord's anointed [meaning kill or hurt King Saul]. (1 Samuel 26:10-11)*

David chose to trust that the Lord would sort it out sooner or later. As far as David knew, King Saul could have chased him for another twenty years. But David was willing to accept that and trust the Lord's judgment and intentions for his life.

In other words, David didn't try to force a solution to his unfair situation. He also didn't rail against God.

If you're inclined to be angry and impatient with the Lord at times, consider the profound scriptures David wrote during his troubled times, as captured in the book of Psalms:

*The Lord is the strength of my life; of whom shall I be afraid? I [would have] fainted, unless I had believed to see the goodness of the Lord. . . .*

*Wait on the Lord: be of good courage, and he shall strengthen thine heart: wait, I say, on the Lord. (Psalm 27:1, 13-14)*

I also "would have fainted" unless I had believed on the goodness of God and stayed close to Him through faith and prayer. "Fainting" in older versions of the Bible refers to running out of energy, being unable to continue, or becoming cowardly. Can you relate to that tendency?

Unfairness is an awful burden to bear alone. Clearly, David did not bear that burden alone.

## Before Joseph Was at the Right Hand of Pharaoh

Here's another story from the Bible of one whose life was wildly unfair. Joseph was the favorite son of Jacob, the Old Testament prophet. In what seems like a tactless act, Jacob gave Joseph a fancy "coat of many colors," but to his other sons, he gave nothing special that we know of.

Hmph. The brothers were miffed and jealous.

Joseph later related to his brothers some of the God-given dreams that, unfortunately, made him appear condescending toward them, which *really* made them mad (see Genesis 37:3–18).

So, his brothers did what any kindhearted group of jealous brothers might do: dug a pit, threw him in, and left him to die. After a while, one of them felt sorry for Joseph, and so they pulled him back out and sold him into slavery instead. Slavery!

Wow.

God eased his burdens for a time by placing him in charge of a wealthy master's household. But when the master's wife (likely very beautiful) kept coming on to Joseph and ultimately grabbed him, saying, "Lie with me," he fled, choosing to respect God and his master instead of giving in to the seductions of his master's wife.

And his reward for such integrity?

The now-angry, jilted woman claimed Joseph had attacked her. Joseph was unfairly thrown into prison and left there for two years (see Genesis chapters 39–41). Ultimately, through a series of miraculous dreams and heavenly opportunities, Joseph was not only released from prison but elevated to the position of Pharaoh's right-hand man.

Here's what Joseph told his brothers years later when they came to Egypt to be saved from starvation due to the famine:

> Be not grieved, nor angry with yourselves, that ye sold me hither: for God did send me before you to preserve life.
>
> . . . God sent me before you to preserve you a posterity in the earth, and to save your lives by a great deliverance.
>
> So now it was not you that sent me hither, but God. (Genesis 45:5-8)

Several fascinating insights from this story are highly relevant to your marriage situation:

- God uses unfair circumstances to work His plans in your life, which very likely will bless others' lives.
- Your spouse should not be overly distressed with himself or herself because of their unfair behavior toward you. That's not to say they should not seek and follow treatment and strive to improve their behavior. Ideally, they should. A growing awareness of their harmful behavior is good and necessary. But a condemning, accusatory stance on your part is always destructive. Your marriage will not prosper if you make your spouse feel like a complete loser and a total drain on the relationship because of his or her problems.

- If God has confirmed the appropriateness of your marriage and you stay faithful to the Lord, He will ultimately turn those experiences to your great blessing. . . probably not as dramatic as becoming the right-hand person to the most powerful ruler in the world, but something wonderfully positive in line with His plan.

## Helen's Perspective

[How she felt years ago]: I totally hate it when Christian tries to tell me I'm being unfair. Give me a break. Everything in my life is unfair, and then he wants me to think about him, like I'm being unfair to *him*? I can't handle it when he says that. I yell at him and tell him I don't want to hear it, and I let him know all the things he does that are unfair to *me*. Besides, it would be obvious to anyone else what he's doing that's unfair to me, and I'm not going to be accused unfairly.

And I really hate it when I express my opinion loudly or with a little passion and then he asks if I've taken my pills this morning. Like everything I say or do is because of my mental health issues! That's totally unfair. Can't I have feelings that are just part of me? The real me? Why does everything have to be my illness?

And why don't I ever make sense to other people? What I'm thinking and trying to say makes perfect sense to me. I'm not trying to be difficult or unfair. But they are unfair when they say I'm not making any sense. I hate that. They should listen and try harder.

[Fast-forward twenty-seven years with effective meds and therapy]: I still get pretty angry when anything seems unfair, but I have learned to be more patient. Feeling empathy for what others are thinking and feeling is still really hard for me even though I am getting better at understanding that people may have made mistakes, have different ways of communicating, I may have taken a comment the wrong way, and things like that.

Nowadays, I think a lot more about Christian's needs, and I often thank him for the many things he does for me, including where my physical disabilities are concerned. He has to do a lot around the house, and he doesn't complain about it being unfair. He just does it, and I respect and appreciate that more than I can possibly say. I tell him all the time, and I know he appreciates that.

I still really dislike it if Christian even implies that I'm being too harsh or angry about something. I think he always thinks I'm having a meltdown or something. But even so, I know he has become afraid and overly sensitive to anger and that I have to respect that and try to create a calm and loving home environment too.

## Jesus and the Joy of Doing Good

The Son of God Himself was repeatedly accused of wrongdoing, deception, plotting against the government, and being possessed by the devil.

Beyond that, in the most unfair act in time and eternity, the perfect, sinless Son of God suffered the pains of all mankind in the Garden of Gethsemane and on the cross of Calvary. There was nothing fair about it. But God the Father willed that it be done for our sake, and Jesus endured it. How could Jesus do it? Consider this amazing scripture:

*Jesus . . . for the joy that was set before him endured the cross. (Hebrews 12:2)*

This is a potent statement.

Jesus endured the grotesque unfairness of the burden of the Atonement and suffered for all who sinned, because of the joy of doing something incredibly important for those He loved.

Joy refers to a deep and lasting happiness that comes from aligning ourselves with God's purposes and thereby accomplishing good and noble things, usually for others. Jesus understood that His paying the price for our sinfulness and foolishness was the only way we could be redeemed and saved in His kingdom. The joy of knowing the good He would be able to offer each of us—personally—is what sustained Him. The scripture says that is how He was able to endure it.

That is a pivotal teaching.

In a very real way, you may be providing a small fraction of that type of Christlike service to your spouse.

Here's a wonderful question to ponder, posed by Russell M. Nelson:

*Joy is powerful, and focusing on joy brings God's power
into our lives. If we focus on the joy that will come to us, or
to those we love, what can we endure that presently seems
overwhelming, painful, scary, unfair, or simply impossible?*[1]

# Hope and Help

## Scriptures to Ponder

*My brethren, count it all joy when you fall into various trials. (James 1:2, NKJV)*

*Blessed is the man that endureth temptation: for when he is tried, he shall receive the crown of life, which the Lord hath promised to them that love him. (James 1:12)*

*For this is thankworthy, if a man for conscience toward God endure grief, suffering wrongfully. For what glory is it, if, when ye be buffeted for your faults, ye shall take it patiently? but if, when ye do well, and suffer for it, ye take it patiently, this is acceptable with God. (1 Peter 2:19-20)*

## What You Can Do Today

- Understand and accept that some aspects of your marriage may not feel completely fair to you—ever.
- Make your relationship with God your highest priority. You need His strength to endure unfairness.
- Understand that your spouse likely feels your relationship is unfair to him or her on some level, whether you believe that's accurate or not. Resist the urge to microanalyze and discuss these different perceptions because such views are typically impossible to resolve with mentally ill individuals who simply perceive the world differently. Instead:
  - At an appropriately calm moment, ask your spouse how he or she feels about a typically controversial question of fairness between the two of you. Then *seek first to understand*, as taught by Steven R. Covey.[2] Covey described being understood by another human as "emotional oxygen." It's that vital. Start by understanding your spouse so he or she can breathe.
  - Then ask your spouse what he or she would like you to do to help or support them. You may prefer that this book defends

*you* and helps you change your spouse. The unfortunate reality is that lasting solutions with a mentally ill person typically require you—the spouse with no issues or fewer issues—to exhibit greater skill and show interest in your spouse's needs, feelings, and perceptions, and then rise to "be the change that you wish to see in the world."[3]

☐ Validate your spouse's feelings as often as possible. If they explain things in nonsensical, unreasonable terms, that makes the conversation more challenging for you, to be sure. Use words that don't condemn but simply say, "That must be hard when (such and such) happens."

☐ Agree to actions you can take that are simple and clear.

☐ If you get a chance to describe your needs and preferences, state them without saying, "You are being unfair to me by doing X." Say, "Such and such things are important to me. It would help me if we can do X in these situations." If you say things like, "I feel like you're being unfair" or "You are stressing me out," the conversation becomes an attack and will go downhill.

## Spiritual Blessings for You

Look forward to these wonderful blessings of patiently persevering with your spouse or loved one in partnership with God.

- Greater humility before God in accepting the lessons on unfairness He has allowed you to experience
- More respect for yourself as you realize you are receiving "advanced training" in Christlike behavior
- Greater maturity and ability to be an example for others at work, in the community, at church, and at home by whining less, manning up, and moving on
- Greater spiritual independence, because you look only to God for confirmation of your thoughts and actions and you don't need humans to validate your actions
- Greater understanding of the character of God as you feel some of the unfair suffering Jesus felt while on earth

# Chapter 6
# My Needs are Not Being Met

**W**e all have legitimate needs, including safety, food, psychological well-being, social relationships, a purpose in life, peace with God, and more.[1]

Yet, consider this paradox Jesus taught:

*Whosoever will save his life shall lose it: and whosoever will lose his life for my sake shall find it. (Matthew 16:25)*

This teaching has puzzled many through the centuries. Did Jesus mean we should forget about our own needs? "Lose his life" sounds absolute. Like 100 percent abandonment. Could that be what Jesus meant?

No. When the challenges in your marriage stretch you to your limits, is it wrong to think, *Hey, wait a minute here. I'm being deprived of (such and such) because of my spouse's behaviors. Shouldn't I consider what I need*?

No, it is not wrong to think that. And it is a misunderstanding if we think we should ignore our basic needs and keep doing everything we can for our spouse until it causes our own collapse. In fact, if you are *not* caring for yourself and developing a strong, healthy sense of self, you will not be able to forge the kind of interdependence a healthy marriage needs. The less strong and healthy you are, the less you have to give.

> 💡 You can't build a healthy marriage of "us" without a healthy "you." Protect and develop your healthy self.

The principle Jesus taught is paraphrased in simpler terms by Gordon B. Hinckley: *He who lives only unto himself withers and dies, while he who forgets himself in the service of others grows and blossoms in this life and in eternity.*[2]

The key clarification here is the phrase "*only* unto himself" (italics added).

It can help to think of "losing yourself" as meaning "losing your *selfishness.*"

Regarding Jesus's lose-your-life expression, in ancient Jewish culture, it was a common practice to exaggerate things to emphasize an important point. In our Western culture—influenced by the rigid logic of mathematics—we often read these biblical teachings too literally. Losing our life does not mean "zero focus" on our own needs, which today's readers might harmfully conclude.[3]

Consider this important warning from mental health professionals for spouses in challenging relationships:

> In many of these situations, caring individuals may think they are insufficiently kind or tolerant. They may blame themselves.
>
> Toxic relationships can lead caring individuals to develop a distorted sense of self-doubt and very problematic Negative Core Beliefs. . . .
>
> Be aware that destructive relationships are highly stressful and take a toll on the five essentials of . . . health, emotions, awareness, relationships, and transcendence.[4]

A deeply spiritual, sincere soul who is striving to do all in her power "for Christ's sake" to save her marriage and help her spouse may "overdo it" if she begins to disregard her own health, emotions, etc. But harming one's self is avoidable through prayer and discernment.

## The Typical Wants of Wives and Husbands

Let's now expand our focus to include both needs *and* wants. The line between needs and wants can be gray, but in general, wants are not as essential to our well-being as are needs. For the remainder of this chapter, let's think of them as both being important to you and your spouse.

Rick Warren's insight below provides a practical perspective for all human relationships, but especially for spouses:

*The mature follower of Jesus stops asking, "Who's going to meet my needs?" and starts asking, "Whose needs can I meet?"*[5]

With the foregoing cautions in mind about how to love others without harming ourselves, let's take a look at two little gems.

Below is a popular top-ten list of what women want from their husbands. This list describes some of the unique things a woman longs for in a relationship.[6]

## What Women Want from Their Husbands

| 1 | To know she's loved through simple daily actions, such as remembering her preferences, small gifts, etc. |
|---|---|
| 2 | Understanding and forgiveness, especially after being moody |
| 3 | Real conversation—not just about the kids, weather, problems |
| 4 | Quality time with you (and the children) |
| 5 | To hear more yes than no when expressing an idea |
| 6 | Better listening skills (not tuning her out or ignoring her) |
| 7 | Affection, kindness, and manners, including gentle touches |
| 8 | Shared household and child-rearing responsibilities |
| 9 | A day off now and then (and dates!) |
| 10 | A healthier attitude about health—in other words, wives want husbands to take better care of themselves. |

Most women reading this will sigh and say, "Yes, oh yes, I love those things." If you're a man, please know that regardless of your wife's mental health issues, these wants don't disappear. Doing your best to fulfill them is a great way to touch her, calm her, and help her feel secure.

Men, consider in particular this important point: if you have grown frustrated with your wife and begun to view her as the source of your affliction, watch out. This judgment inevitably comes out in how you speak to her (e.g., the tone of your voice, the quickness of your irritation, or the coolness of your interactions). As you saw in chapter 3: "I'm Starting to Doubt Myself and My Faith," there's a big difference between the bride you love and the illness that afflicts her.

Don't underestimate her need for genuine kindness. Tenderness is so important. Reconsider the importance of being nice. The rest of this book will help you gain the strength to be nice and tender and kind, even after all you have been through. If you don't, all your other efforts can be blown to the wind because her need for kindness cries so loudly from within her.

Now, let's look at what men want from their wives.[7]

## What Men Want from Their Wives

| 1 | Affection (and yes, sex, but this is about truly liking him) |
|---|---|
| 2 | Belief in his abilities |
| 3 | Understanding (you "get" him) |
| 4 | Appreciation and affirmation of his work and efforts |
| 5 | Acceptance and allowing for differences of opinion/tastes |
| 6 | Less chatter (at times) |
| 7 | Respect, listening to him, and taking him seriously |
| 8 | Free time, both in and out of the house |
| 9 | Trust |
| 10 | Companionship/friendship |

Again, most men reading this will think, "Well, yeah. That's it exactly." Regardless of mental issues, a marriage will be stronger and happier when a wife does her best to address these wants in addition to dealing with mental health behaviors.

As a man, I can tell you that this list is spot-on. From my own experience and from hearing countless men tell me about the stress in their marriages, I can tell you that men need to feel your admiration regarding the things they do well. Expressing appreciation relieves their stress and pumps them with a bit of energy. Constant criticism drains them. Lack of space, quiet, and free time become suffocating. Focusing on just one or two of the items on this list can work wonders for how your challenging spouse feels.

## And This Is a Hopeful Message?

You may feel like we've added more to your already overflowing bucket of responsibilities. In a way, we have.

But in two big ways, these lists of wants can be stress-relieving. They are meant to keep you grounded in the realities that exist within every marriage plus give you ideas to explore in prayer and in conversation with your spouse.

1. You will find that to varying degrees, depending on the severity of your spouse's condition, addressing your spouse's typical male or female wants and needs will prevent or diffuse conflict. Mentally ill spouses flare up when they are under stress. And when are they under stress? When they perceive that their needs (or wants) are not being met.
2. If these lists resonate with you, find an opportunity to discuss them in a moment of calm. First, ask your spouse to identify which are most important to them. Then pick one or two that are particularly important for you. You may have never thought of how to describe your wants with words. Some of the items on these lists may jump out at you and help you explain your feelings.

A word of caution: some individuals get triggered and stressed out when their spouse asks for something. In an instant, their thought process becomes: "My spouse wants X, but I may not be able to give X, so he will hate me and then divorce me, and I will be all alone. I knew it. He is just setting me up because he wants a divorce." (This is common for the BPD spouse.) Unfortunately, anticipating negative reactions or misinterpretations is what a spouse in such a situation must do. If you are as loving, reassuring, and gentle as possible, it will increase the chances that the conversation goes well.

Does thinking about your spouse's needs add to your burden? Sure it does, in a way. But over time, can such conversations lead to greater understanding and change, ultimately lightening your burden? Yes, they can, and they do.

## Helen's Perspective

[How she would have felt years ago]: When my husband starts talking about what he needs or even hints that he hasn't been getting what he needs, it makes me feel terribly guilty. All I hear in my mind is, *You're no good for him. There are other women who would take better care of him and make him happier. Lots of them. You should just die and let him get on with a better life.*

Besides, why is he talking about *his* needs? I'm the one who isn't getting my needs met. He's always working or doing stuff for church and never wants to spend any time with me. He never buys me anything anymore. I never have anybody. I have nothing!

He wants somebody perfect. Nobody can do everything he wants, certainly not me.

[Fast-forward twenty-seven years]: Looking back, I really did feel like I had nothing, and I said those very words many times. I was so desperately miserable at those times that I couldn't see any blessings. Everything was just horribly miserable. My husband tried hard a lot of times. It was impossible to make me happy all the time. When he tried something special, the boost to my mood only lasted a few days, and then I would feel dark and alone again and forget all about it. If he reminded me of something he had done for me to help me think more "fairly," I would completely lose it because it made me feel guilty. He honestly couldn't win those conversations if he tried to "straighten out" my thinking.

I will say that it did help when he would cancel commitments to help me on a bad day. He would also cut back on church service and helping other people so he could spend as much time with me as possible. I really, really needed his time. I need to talk to people a lot, and I lose my mind when there's nobody to talk to.

I tried to do better at giving him free time. For a few weeks or a month here and there, it went pretty well, like encouraging him to go to yoga one night a week or to go fishing. He appreciated it and said it helped. And even though I had dark days, over time, I started to believe he was really trying to be good to me too. When I felt better, I felt guilty at the same time because I started to see how rotten I had been. That was the hard part about getting better. It was hard to realize how all he was doing was giving because of my problems and I could hardly give anything consistently.

## The Five Love Languages

No need is more fundamental than the need to feel loved.

Let's look at five different ways to fulfill the need for love in a marriage based on the research and advice of Dr. Gary Chapman in his best-selling *The 5 Love Languages: The Secret to Love that Lasts*. This is powerful stuff because it is so simple to apply.

In Dr. Chapman's words, everyone has a tank—a love tank.[8] If the tank is full or mostly full, we feel more at peace in our marriages. If it's empty or nearly empty, we're dissatisfied and feel stressed.

Spouses usually have different ways of filling their tanks. Unfortunately, our spouses don't come with an instruction manual that tells us how to fill those tanks. We're often blind to it, even in ourselves.

The good news is that research has shown that every man and woman has one of five primary ways—called "love languages"—they prefer to experience love in their relationships. If we can identify a person's preferred love language, we're halfway home. Here they are:

| Love Preference | What It Looks Like |
| --- | --- |
| Words of Affirmation | Compliments, encouragement, a kind and empathetic manner of speaking, etc. |
| Quality Time | Devoted, undistracted time spent in conversation, effective listening, or happily doing something with the spouse that is meaningful to *them* |
| Receiving Gifts | Willingly, unexpectedly presented objects, words, or sacrifices of time that say, "I was thinking of you and what you like." |

| Love Preference | What It Looks Like |
|---|---|
| Service Rendered | Completing chores, special projects, household responsibilities, and personal favors that are important to the spouse, either personally or with others (the kids) |
| Physical Touch | Sitting close, touching, holding hands, massaging, sex that is mutually satisfying |

We might look at this list and think, "That's common sense. Everyone likes all that stuff."

Well, maybe not. What you may not know is that your spouse prefers one of these five love languages over the others. His or her greatest frustrations (and yours) are probably caused by their not receiving enough of their primary need for that type of love. As Dr. Chapman describes it,

> Your love language and the language of your spouse may be as different as Chinese from English. No matter how hard you try to express love in English, if your spouse understands only Chinese, you will never understand how to love each other.[9]

In other words, you may be an expert at words of affirmation. You may try all day long to say positive and encouraging things, but your spouse may crave quality time over everything and you're not really sure how to do that. You may think you're spending quality time with them, but you may be missing what that really means. You're thinking one way, and your spouse is thinking another. The variations of such mismatches of love languages are endless. Read *The 5 Love Languages* for examples and crystal-clear insights. It's brilliant, short, and eye-opening.

## Talk about It

Identifying and exploring your spouse's preferred language is best done when they are not in crisis. They will likely appreciate your proactive focus on them. Pray, prepare, and approach this topic in the simplest, most nonthreatening way possible.

Perhaps you can say something like, "I recently read that spouses prefer to be loved in different ways. Which of these do you think is the most important to you?" Then list the five things from a notepad or off the top of your head and listen. If you approach this conversation with the genuine intention to understand your spouse as opposed to getting them to understand you, you'll experience more success.

If they ask about your preferred love language, be gentle and watch for the tendency to release the flood gates that have been holding back your pent-up frustration and start unloading all you've been missing out on.

If the conversation fails because your spouse feels threatened or starts "throwing in the kitchen sink," so be it. You tried in good faith. But keep this love-tank model in mind, try to discern your spouse's preferences on your own, and just start doing better at it.

Another word of warning: mentally troubled individuals and substance abusers can be skilled manipulators who take advantage of a spouse's best intentions to meet their needs. When striving to fill your spouse's love tank, consider:

> Allowing oneself to be used or manipulated by another is not an act of love. It is, in fact, an act of treason. You are allowing him or her to develop inhumane habits. Love says, "I love you too much to let you treat me this way. It is not good for you or me."[10]

We continue the topic of avoiding manipulation in chapter 8, "My Spouse is Walking All Over Me," where we explore ways to set limits and boundaries on your spouse's behaviors.

## Perspective: What Will Harm You Spiritually?

So far, we've considered the needs and wants common to men and women as well as five ways spouses feel loved in their relationships.

Realistically, of course, you may do your best to fulfill your spouse's wants and needs for love, but your spouse may not do the same for you. You may repeatedly give your best but not see your spouse's behaviors improving, at least for now.

That's hard. But does it mean your marriage is over and your efforts are wasted?

No.

One goal of this book is to help you thrive, spiritually speaking. For you to move from surviving to thriving, you need to separate the less-important needs in life from the critically important, spiritual needs. Take a moment and consider how you might answer these questions in the context of your relationship:

- If we (meaning you and your spouse) are tight on money and have different priorities, does that harm me spiritually?
- If my spouse gets angry after we see my ex-spouse while we're out shopping, does that harm me spiritually?
- If my spouse seems distant and doesn't listen well when I talk, even though I've asked him to do better, does that harm me spiritually?
- If I want more free time with no strings attached, but I haven't been getting it for years, does that harm me spiritually?
- If my spouse refuses to seek professional help or follow advice from professionals, does that harm me spiritually?

The answer to these questions is no.

You won't be harmed with respect to your spiritual growth. You will be under additional stress, to be sure. And that stress could influence you to make bad decisions and act sinfully. But the stress-causing behavior will not in itself harm your spiritual growth—meaning your development of a more Christlike character.

Would life be more pleasant and enjoyable if those stressors didn't exist? Absolutely, and it's perfectly reasonable to hope for less stress. We all would prefer that our wants and needs are met in a more complete way. But that may not happen in this life.

What *will* harm you spiritually is avoiding the challenges God has given you.

What will harm you is making poor decisions under stress, like engaging in escapist, sinful behavior (e.g., pornography, drinking, binge-anything) or developing a rash tongue, hasty temper, or attempting to control or force your spouse to "face reality" and change.

Those behaviors *will* harm you spiritually.

Your spouse's inability or refusal to meet your needs will not harm you unless they become abusive or begin to destroy your ability to earn income, stay healthy, care for your family, etc.

## Perspective: What Does It Mean to Thrive Spiritually?

Let's take a look at what it means to thrive spiritually. The standard definitions of *thrive* are:

1. To grow or develop vigorously
2. To prosper or flourish

Synonyms of *thrive* include *prosper, blossom, advance, make strides,* and *succeed.*[11]

Everything in this book is focused on helping you thrive in your eternal purpose and God's plan for your life and, by extension, the well-being of your family. So, if our very purpose in life is to grow spiritually and in "Christ-likeness," our greatest need is to live within the conditions that lead to spiritual growth.

For example, if you want your flowers or garden plants to thrive, you know they will need water, good soil, fertilizer, sunlight, space to expand, absence of pests, etc. Your challenges are like Miracle-Gro®, the super fertilizer that's like steroids for veggies!

> 💡 True growth requires a life full of challenges and increasingly complex problems that help you learn to make good decisions, follow Christ more fully, and consistently reject evil.

## Development of Christlike Love

The preceding sections may have seemed harsh or unfair to you. People in your life are probably saying things like, "You shouldn't have to live like that," or "When are you ever going to get what *you* need?"

From God's perspective, however, you may be getting exactly what you need to thrive *spiritually*. Growing spiritually often requires sacrifice or at least a deferment of less-important needs and wants.

The greatest spiritual attribute any of us can acquire in this life is Christlike love. Remember what the Bible says: "The greatest of these is love" (1 Corinthians 13:13). Think about the love Christ has for us as described in the chart below, then pray about how His example of love relates to your challenging situation. Ponder these for a good, long while.

| Christ's Example | How Can You Follow It? |
|---|---|
| Jesus paid attention to others' circumstances and needs. He was so aware and concerned that He would stop what He was doing. | |
| Jesus thought and cared about the needs of others more than His own. He frequently served and served for long, tiring days on end. | |
| Jesus was willing to endure the pain caused by others and their poor choices. Whether suffering from harsh words or angry tones that were not justified, He endured it. Lastly, He paid the excruciating price for our sins—even though He had done no wrong. | |

## Codependency: An Important Caution

Please don't think your best efforts to meet your spouse's wants and needs will "fix" them and make their mental health or addictive behaviors go away.

In the 1980s, there emerged a new concept called "codependency," which originally described an unhealthy condition of spouses married to alcoholics.[12] In clinical terms, codependency is the opposite of "differentiation," which is the ability to maintain a distinct, healthy sense of self as you interact with family members, friends, and even institutions. Instead of being distinct or different, the codependent spouse becomes enmeshed and intertwined in very unhealthy ways.

Codependent spouses allow themselves to get caught up in the insanity of their addicted spouse's thinking and behavior—all in the name of trying to "help them." They go to any length possible to keep liquor away from their spouses and to keep them from ruining their family's lives. Yet, they often back down and accommodate behaviors that make them feel utterly violated.

The consequences are tragic. The well-meaning spouse drives themselves mad trying to accomplish the impossible. The term *codependent* suggests that the spouse gets sucked into their spouse's alcohol dependency, even though they are not an alcoholic themselves. They lose their own sense of self while trying to control and manipulate their spouses.

If substance abuse or pornography addiction are the primary issues in your relationship, we recommend you seek out resources to help you understand the dynamics of addiction and the recovery process.

Know that the recommendations in this book are balanced in light of research on codependency. You will also see that God is most certainly not codependent in His approach to loving and saving us. So please believe these things:

- You are allowed to think for yourself and have your own opinions, which may be opposite your spouse's views.
- You can't give and give so much that your spouse will be "fixed."
- You cannot control, change, or fix your spouse.
- You will experience hardships along with and often caused by your spouse, and probably for a long time.
- You may give all you possibly can, and your spouse will still make harmful decisions that are not your fault.
- You must be willing to allow your spouse to choose wrongly and experience their own painful consequences.

One of the solutions to codependency, it turns out, is setting healthy boundaries to protect your needs. (See chapter 8, "My Spouse is Walking All Over Me")

## Fifty-Fifty or 100 Percent?

So, how much should you give? How much is too much? Although I hear it less lately, some people still give this bad advice to young married couples: "Marriage is fifty-fifty. You both have to give."

This advice is problematic in three ways:

1.  Both spouses should give their 100 percent best effort, not just 50 percent while expecting the other to add their 50 percent. In marriage it's not addition, it's multiplication. Two halves don't make a whole, they make a quarter. In order to have a whole, healthy marriage, you have to have two whole, healthy people.

2.  We can't control what our spouses do, so it is pointless to get frustrated if you think your spouse is giving less than their 100 percent. Yes, both *should* give 100 percent, but since you can only control how well *you* are giving, it's best to close your eyes a bit when it comes to measuring your spouse's giving. You'll be happiest if you focus on your 100 percent and leave your spouse's behavior in God's hands.

3.  You may think you know your spouse's whole situation and all their motives, but life is far more complex than we realize, and to the end of our days, we won't ever know the depth of another person's struggles and full situation. If you try to assess whether your spouse is trying hard enough, you will run into trouble because you can't understand his or her world. Mental and emotional problems are like a maze neither of you really understands. You don't know your spouse's limitations and therefore can't accurately judge.

## A Word about Chastity

It's likely the turmoil in your relationship has affected your sexual and emotional intimacy with your spouse. Typically, and understandably, you long for both forms of intimacy.

But what if your needs are not being met? Whether there's intentional withholding of sex or lack of emotional intimacy because of the chaos and hard feelings, it's not uncommon that a spouse is drawn into the temptation of seeking emotional comfort or outright sexual affairs.

Is it a big deal? Yes, both flirting and sexual affairs are a big deal.

The topic of sex must be very important if we consider how often God has given commandments, counsel, and punishments regarding sexual behavior. The Bible contains literally hundreds of warnings regarding sexual thoughts and behavior. Immorality is a grievous sin.

The opposite of adultery is fidelity, which means faithfulness. But another word—less common today—is chastity.

Sometimes we mistakenly think of chastity as abstinence from sex. This is not correct. The Latin root of the word *chastity* means "purity." The Russian tradition calls it the "wisdom of wholeness."[13] Chastity is most certainly a positive virtue and blessing, even if you suspect you are behaving in a more chaste manner than your spouse.

You cannot have God's full measure of inspiration and strength if you "split yourself" and become "unwhole" by developing a romantic relationship with another person or fantasize about relationships with countless others via pornography. Unchaste behavior is a prime example of what Jesus meant when He said, "Satan hath desired to have you, that he may sift you as wheat" (see Luke 22:31).

If your needs for intimacy are not being met in your marriage, don't let your mind create excuse-making scriptural footnotes, like, "Thou shalt not commit adultery [except when my marriage gets really difficult]," (Exodus 21:14) or "Whosoever looketh on a woman [for lust or emotional sustenance] hath [not] committed adultery with her already in his heart" (Matthew 5:28).

Your need to stay pure and whole and chaste remains strong as ever. We encourage you to pray carefully about this and not entrap yourself in a situation that will surely lead to foul consequences for you and a faster decline in your marriage. Our challenge—and it is a great one—is to be wholly, purely, faithfully devoted to our spouses in every way, including chastity. Yes, even when our needs are not being met.

As with all righteous objectives in life, we should not try to accomplish them alone. Going solo is foolishness, and we won't succeed. God wants you to come to Him in your weakness and draw upon His grace with humility, as captured so beautifully by Sarah Young, written as if Jesus is speaking to you:

> *Your weakness does not repel Me. On the contrary, it attracts My Power, which is always available to flow into a yielded heart. Do not condemn yourself for your constant need of help. Instead, come to Me with your gaping neediness; let the Light of My Love fill you.*[14]

## Losing "Yourself-ishness" Is a Blessing

Let's revisit the inspired ground we've covered in this chapter:

1. Our natural tendency to serve only ourselves can be replaced by making it a priority to serve our spouse. Selfishness can decrease, and Christlike love can increase.
2. "Forgetting ourselves" does not mean abandoning our fundamental needs for safety, health, and happiness.
3. Wives and husbands have unique wants. We reduce our own stress in a relationship when we become better at noticing and fulfilling our spouse's wants.
4. All humans need love but have strong preferences for how that love is shown. We can greatly increase joy in our marriage by identifying the kind of love our spouse needs most.
5. Complex problems in your marriage are like MiracleGro® for the soul.
6. Developing Christlike love is the ultimate outcome of successfully working through difficult spiritual challenges.
7. Marriage is a 100/100 percent relationship, not 50/50. You will find greater peace if you focus on your 100 percent, but you do not have to give 110 percent.
8. Chastity matters. Watch out for excuse making.

What do all the above have in common? They lead us to the abandonment of selfishness, the real enemy in all marriages.

What will happen to us as we seek this radical change through the Holy Spirit? Here's a promise from Timothy Keller:

> *People with a deep grasp of the gospel can turn around and admit that their selfishness is the problem and that they're going to work on it. And when they do that, they will often discover an immediate sense of liberation, of waking up from a troubling dream.*[15]

# Hope and Help

## Scriptures to Ponder

*Husbands, love your wives, even as Christ also loved the church, and gave himself for it . . . let every one of you in particular so love his wife even as himself; and the wife see that she reverence her husband. (Ephesians 5:25, 33)*

*"By this shall all men know that ye are my disciples, if ye have love one to another." (John 13:35)*

*Let us run with patience the race that is set before us, looking unto Jesus, the author and finisher of our faith; who for the joy that was set before him endured the cross. (Hebrews 12:1-2)*

## What You Can Do Today

- Strive to mentally separate your spouse's normal wants and needs from the needs related to their condition.
- Discuss the five love languages in the most simple, nonthreatening way possible.
  - Start like this: "I recently read that spouses prefer to be loved in different ways. Which of these do you think is the most important to you?"
  - If you approach this conversation with a genuine intention to understand your spouse as opposed to getting them to understand you, you'll experience more success. If the timing seems right, share your preference.
- Perhaps you've told yourself it isn't fair that you give so much when your needs aren't being met. Ask yourself if you've been holding back from giving 100 percent.

## Spiritual Blessings for You

Look forward to these wonderful blessings of patiently persevering with your spouse or loved one in partnership with God.

- Recognition that you are not being spiritually harmed; you are being given MiracleGro®

- Greater recognition that people are fundamentally different in what they like, want, and need
- Greater appreciation for God's incredibly loving nature and wisdom in dealing with you
- Greater commitment to following Jesus's example of loving everyone around Him, even when they were difficult to love

## Chapter 7

# I'm Totally Drained and Afraid

**N**ot many years ago, I felt like I had truly reached the end of my ability to cope with the continuing difficulties in our marriage. It was year twenty-six.

After experiencing yet another torturously unfair, conversational vortex, I wanted to smash my fist through the wall. I didn't. I went downstairs, bent down and pounded the seat of a chair as I roared out a primal "Argh!" and inwardly pled for heaven to give me the strength to get through that moment.

I was running out of steam and approaching panic. My mental fatigue was bone-deep, plus my job was intensely challenging at the time. In spite of God's guidance and everything I had invested emotionally and arranged in our lives financially, I feared I had backed myself into an inescapable corner. Was God allowing everything to collapse after all this time?

Why were my pain and fatigue so deep? From the first year of our marriage, we had had emotionally intense arguments.

Imagine the nights when my wife couldn't calm down and kept fussing and poking and saying irrational things to the point where all hope of sleep vanished and I still had to work the next day. At times I called out of work more often than I should have, straining my relationship with my employers. When I was at work, I felt the weight of my own mental issues pressing down on me, making me evasive and reducing my available energy for others. But what could I say about what I was experiencing? Only a select few knew anything about what I was going through.

This went on year after unbelievable year. Five, then ten, then fifteen, then twenty. Twenty-five? Really? *Still?*

The improvements in our relationship had been real, but so was my declining ability to deal with emotional and mental turmoil.

I felt my mind physically changing. The effects of age? Prolonged trauma? I wasn't sure. But I felt my stamina waning thin. Here we were, at year twenty-six, and I was in tatters with only a pinhole of hope remaining.

I didn't know it at the time, but Helen was about to be admitted to a treatment program that dramatically improved our lives. That was about one month after this incident. We never know those kinds of things in advance, so what can we do when we run out of steam?

We turn to God, often because we have nowhere else to turn. We may have tried hard on our own, perhaps with many prayers but without truly drinking from the Fountain of Living Waters. Some have heard the words "draw strength from God," but they aren't sure how to do that.

Without truly finding sustenance in God, many give up on their marriages or do rash and violent things out of exhaustion and fear. When you feel backed into a corner and out of options, it's terrifying, isn't it?

I praise God that I discovered how to fully receive His lifting, loving power, right during this critical time in my life. The following Bible story is a rich and powerful metaphor that illustrates how this can happen for you.

## The Story of Abigail and David[1]

Many Bible readers are unaware of the beautiful Old Testament story of Abigail, who was the wife of a nasty, ungrateful man named Nabal. The symbolic meaning of this story is so powerful that once I understood and applied it, I never felt helplessly drained again.

At the time of this story, David was not yet king of Israel, although he had been anointed to become king by the prophet Samuel (see 1 Samuel 16). David had about six hundred men following him at the time and was frequently chased and harassed by King Saul, who for no valid reason decided to make David his enemy, as we discussed in chapter 5: "It's Not Fair." (See 1 Samuel chapters 19–24)

David was fed up and weary. Unfortunately, he ended up getting mistreated yet again by Nabal, who was described by his servants and wife as a "son of the devil" and such a wicked fool that "a man cannot speak to him" (1 Samuel 25:17, 25).

On a certain day, David's hungry army of six hundred needed food, so he sent some of his men to ask Nabal's servants for supplies. It's clear from the biblical account that David had previously been kind to them and provided them protection. But now David had a critical need.

When the servants asked Nabal, he railed against David and basically told them, "No way. I don't owe him anything." (See 1 Samuel 25:10–11)

That was it. David snapped. He directed his men:

*"Each of you strap on your sword!" So they did,*
*and David strapped his on as well.*

*"May God deal with David, be it ever so severely, if by morning I leave*
*alive one male of all who belong to him!" (1 Samuel 25:13, 22, NIV)*

David intended to wipe out Nabal and all of his male family members and servants. He'd had it. No more!

Unknown to David, Nabal's beautiful and intelligent wife had heard of her husband's rudeness and David's plan to attack. She quickly gathered supplies and, with her servants and food offerings going before her, approached David like this:

*And when Abigail saw David, she hasted, and lighted off the ass, and*
*fell before David on her face, and bowed herself to the ground, and fell*
*at his feet, and said, "Upon me, my lord, upon me let this iniquity*
*be: and let thine handmaid, I pray thee, speak in thine audience,*
*and hear the words of thine handmaid." (1 Samuel 25:23-24)*

At this pivotal moment in the story, Abigail becomes a symbol of Jesus Christ—He who can make us whole when others have wronged us, He who fills us with strength when we are depleted, He who intercedes when we are tempted to act foolishly.

As you continue to read, imagine yourself in that moment just like David—repeatedly hurt and wronged, fed up, hungry, and sick of the whole situation—and then picture the Savior instead of Abigail, bent on the ground in front of *you*.

Photo by Godworld. Used with permission.

## The Savior Bows Down with Grace before Us

Is it wrong to think of Jesus bowing before us with gifts to make us whole? Certainly not, given that He taught, *"Whoever will be greatest among you, let him be your servant"* (see Matthew 23:11). Incredibly, He who knelt and washed the feet of His apostles also bows at our feet with gifts of love, compassion, understanding, and strength to make us whole.

> If you have any feelings of anger or violence in you, do they not melt away as you see God lower Himself in front of you—the very picture of humility? Does this not bring you to your own knees before Him?

Let's continue the story. After kneeling before David, Abigail looked up and said:

> Let this gift [meaning all the food and supplies], which
> your servant has brought to my lord, be given to the
> men who follow you. (1 Samuel 25:27, NIV)

David was deeply touched. Finally, some compassion and tangible help! Not only did Abigail meet his army's physical needs, she prevented a horrific crime and the guilty conscience that would have followed David for life. His heart was softened as he answered her:

> Blessed be the Lord God of Israel, which sent thee this day to
> meet me. And blessed be thy advice, and blessed be thou, which
> hast kept me this day from coming to shed blood, and from
> avenging myself with mine own hand. (1 Samuel 25:32-33)

## When You Are Nearly Empty

You, like David, may be looking to your spouse, symbolized by Nabal, to meet your desperate yet reasonable needs.

*Isn't that what spouses are for?* you may think. *Can't I expect something from him now and then? Especially after everything I have to deal with?*

This type of thinking is flawed, however. Even in "normal" marriages, too many spouses expect their partners to be their emotional savior, to fill them with good feelings and energy, improve their self-esteem, make them happy, and more.

While these blessings often accompany stable marriages, the idea that we get them primarily from our spouses is utterly out of sync with the biblical view of marriage. That's not our partner's role.

The kind of deep and foundational fulfillment we crave most in our lives can come only from God, even though modern culture says you don't need God for that. Modern culture says, "All you need is the right, compatible companion to be happy." But this philosophy is false and barking up the wrong tree.

The story of David and Abigail is a powerful metaphor for how Jesus Christ will give you what your spouse can't give you and wasn't ever meant to give you, spiritually speaking. Only God can give you what you need on that deepest level. Consider this profoundly important quote by Timothy Keller:

> The gospel can . . . give you an internal fullness that frees you to be generous with [your spouse] even when you are not getting the satisfaction you want out of the relationship.
>
> Without the help of the Spirit, without a continual refilling of your soul's tank with the glory and love of the Lord, such submission to the interests of the other is virtually impossible to accomplish for any length of time without becoming resentful.
>
> I call this "love economics." You can only afford to be generous if you actually have some money in the bank to give.[2]

## Helen's Perspective

[How she would have felt years ago]: When I sense that my husband is worn out and depressed, it makes me feel guilty and scared. I hate when he acts like that. I go into a downward spiral of self-hate and guilt-induced anger, and I usually say mean things to him.

It scares me when he gets tired because he's more likely to say and do whatever he feels like, such as leaving me. It's just a matter of time until he hurts me again. I know he's eventually going to leave me anyway, so when he acts tired or depressed, I say mean things just to see if he really loves me. If he really loves me, he won't get angry or leave me. He should love me unconditionally, tired or not. Isn't that what a husband should do? What about *my* fears and feelings? Don't I count?

[Fast-forward twenty-seven years]: Just one month prior to entering a long-term treatment facility in Pittsburgh, I was still blaming my husband for everything—not all the time but often. I had had a complete meltdown and was in a local psychiatric hospital again. I was fuming mad the whole time. I sensed the staff believed what my husband was saying more than they believed me. I hated it when people didn't believe what I was saying, like I was always wrong and misunderstanding everything.

But when I finally started dialectical behavior therapy (DBT) and they started me on more effective medications, I began to be more open. In one group-therapy session, I admitted I was a source of a lot of our problems. The people in my group couldn't believe I'd said that. They all thought other people were the problem in their lives too. "We never heard anyone say that," they said.

I started saying I had been unfair to my husband. I hadn't let him feel safe when he said he was worn out. He had a right to be tired and a right to rest. I hadn't respected that because I was afraid of what he would do.

I tend to think in black and white. Either I'm 100 percent right and you're 100 percent wrong or the other way around. I've learned to see gray areas and become open to the fact that both of us might be a little worn out. Both of us might be a little wrong. Both of us might feel a little unloved. I've learned how to monitor my feelings and thoughts and question whether they are fair.

## Trust in Christ More Than in Other Remedies and Escapes

You've probably tried to find relief from your suffering marriage in many ways before today.

Your **positive** efforts might have included

- Scripture reading
- Church attendance
- Praying
- Self-help books
- Browsing information online
- Recommendations from counselors
- Talking to supportive friends for empathy and relaxing conversation.

Your **negative** efforts might have included

- Spending money
- Endless hours of video games, internet, and TV
- Avoiding home and spouse
- Burying yourself in work
- Food or substance abuse
- Flirting or getting emotionally involved with another person
- Pornography or worse

> ☀ We tend to look to anything but God to cope with our troubles.

The positive efforts above are useful and will ideally lead you to God's power. But if you have not yet experienced the very real, spiritual power of Christ, you have missed out on your greatest source of relief.

If you wonder whether you have experienced this lifting, loving, godly power, you probably have not.

Even attending church, reading scriptures, and praying can fail to provide real power if you have not genuinely connected to Jesus Christ as your God and Savior.

If the story of Abigail strikes you as a nice intellectual metaphor but offers no hope of relief, please think about it again. Perhaps you have not yet discovered how to experience Christ as a real, undeniable source of power that comforts and fills your inner being with renewed strength.

## What It Means to Believe in Jesus

Each of us must believe first and foremost in God and "in Jesus Christ, whom [He] has sent" (see John 17:3).

If you're thinking, *I already believe in Jesus*, that's positive, of course, but let's think a little deeper. Believing is a far more action-oriented, committed state of the heart than we may realize.

> ☀ The Greek word *pisteuo*, translated in our Bible as "believe," actually refers to a combination of "believe, trust, and obey."[3]

God wants you to look to Jesus with spiritual, inner eyes and a heart wide open and full of belief as your *first* source of life and hope. Look to Him before all other remedies and escapes.

This book would be three times as long if we were to list all the scriptures that teach us to praise and thank God as our first love, our most trusted partner, our Savior and refuge from the frightening storms and troubles of life.[4] Those aren't just words. Learning to live with a spirit of praise and thanksgiving is key to living with less fear (see also chapter 12, "Joyful After All" for more on managing fear).

It all starts by looking to Jesus through the lens of belief.

You can pray something like this, but in your own thoughts and words: "Dear Father, please save me from this hell and exhaustion I'm feeling. I want to do the right thing, but I need energy and someone to just love, understand, and help me. Please be my refuge. I'm willing to stop looking to my negative escapes and other helpers first. I want to look to you first. Help me in the strugglings of my heart to believe and trust you first. I am willing. I am. I believe that good things will follow."

Despite your concerns about an uncertain future, as you experience the influx of comfort that comes from Christ, I testify that these words from Rick Warren will be true for you:

*When life doesn't make sense, we can still have peace.*[5]

# Hope and Help

## Scriptures to Ponder

*Though I walk through the valley of the shadow of death, I will fear no evil: for thou art with me. (Psalm 23:4)*

*But my God shall supply all your need according to his riches in glory by Christ Jesus. (Philippians 4:19)*

*"But seek ye first the kingdom of God, and his righteousness; and all these things shall be added unto you." (Matthew 6:33)*

*And the peace of God, which passeth all understanding, shall keep your hearts and minds through Christ Jesus. (Philippians 4:7)*

Note: The Greek word *phrourēsei* translated above as "keep" is rich. It means to "watch in advance," "guard," or "protect." What does that mean for you, seeing that the "peace of God" can actually protect you?

## What You Can Do Today

- Identify at least one thing you have turned to for relief more than Jesus Christ. What or who do you believe/trust/obey as a source of energy and comfort more than the Lord of heaven and earth, your creator?
- Decide or recommit to centering your "spiritual eyes" and confidence on Jesus Christ, "whom God sent" to save you amid your current predicament (John 6:29).
- If you feel the metaphor of David and Abigail is too "fuzzy" for you to make it real for yourself, do you know someone who is well connected to God in their hardships of life, someone you can go to for advice and insight on how they got connected?

## Spiritual Blessings for You

Look forward to these wonderful blessings of patiently persevering with your spouse or loved one in partnership with God.

- A deeper understanding of spiritual grace to feed your needs
- More reliance on God—the one we are commanded to rely upon
- More naturally flowing words of praise and gratitude toward God for the simplest of blessings

# Chapter 8

# My Spouse Is Walking All Over Me!

I recall sitting in a therapy session and describing a recurrent dream. We had never talked about dreams before, but this one flashed into my memory as I talked about how out of control my life felt.

My wonderful therapist smiled with the greatest joy each time I achieved a breakthrough of some kind. Suddenly he was beaming at me.

"It's a simple dream, but it's so frustrating," I said. "I'm driving a car down the road, and I'm trying to slow down, but the brake pedal is always just a little out of reach. I stretch my leg and toes as far as I can, but I can never press down. I can touch the pedal, but I can't press it to make the car slow down."

He nodded, still smiling.

"This isn't rocket science, is it?" I asked.

He shook his head.

"I'm stuck in a car that's driving itself, and I feel helpless to stop it."

He nodded with approval.

"Yeah, that's definitely how I feel." I sighed.

Within months of this conversation, I improved in my ability to set boundaries and take control of my life, and I began to feel better.

## Our Right and Responsibility to Act for Ourselves

You have both the right and responsibility to control your life and take care of yourself *first*. This is not selfish. It's actually a God-given expectation (see Numbers 33:51–52 and Matthew 23:26).

There is a great difference between being self-centered and caring for yourself. A mentally ill or addicted spouse can walk all over you for years if you don't learn the art of boundary setting.

Boundary experts Henry Cloud and John Townsend explain why boundaries are so important:

> Boundaries define us. They define what is me and what is not me. A boundary shows me where I end and where someone else begins, leading me to sense of ownership. . . .
>
> In addition to showing us what we are responsible for, boundaries help us to define what is not on our property and what we are not responsible for.
>
> We are not, for example, responsible for other people. Nowhere are we commanded to have "other-control," although we spend a lot of time and energy trying to get it.[1]

The Bible teaches a lot about "self"-control, but it also teaches a lot about dealing with others. The Bible describes how to *respond* appropriately to others, *influence* them, *love* them, and *be true* to our commitments to others—but not how to *control* others.

Until you become clear about what you need, what you are willing to tolerate from others, and then act accordingly, you will feel like I did—strapped into a car driven by itself and unable to stop it.

💡 Setting boundaries did more to save our marriage than anything except our faith in God.

Yet setting boundaries is what we tend to fear the most. Why? Because unstable people hate boundaries, especially substance abusers. Every time we tell our spouse no or say, "This is what I really need to take care of myself," we risk experiencing major conflict, so we tend to back down and accept whatever is intolerable and making us miserable.

Then we kick ourselves for selling out on our own needs.

## God, the People of Israel, and You

Many struggle with the ethics of boundaries. *Is it really right to take a stand like this?* they wonder. "What if my spouse does (such and such bad thing) as a result of me setting a boundary? Isn't it selfish of me? Jesus wouldn't do that, would He?"

Jesus would take a stand, and did, many times.

We can learn much about "What would Jesus do?" by studying the Old Testament. After all, Jesus Christ was the God who spoke to Moses. Let's not forget that (see Isaiah 43:11 and John 8:48–59).

One of the most fascinating things about the Old Testament is that the story of God's dealings with the people of Israel is astonishingly parallel to our experiences with God as we walk through life. In this comparison, you will see these two important truths illustrated:

> 💡 God sets boundaries with His people and enforces them. God expects us to set and enforce boundaries to protect and bless ourselves.

The left column summarizes the history of the people of Israel, which you will likely recognize as the main storyline of the Old Testament. The right column describes how this story relates to our life experiences.

| God and the People of Israel | How This Relates to Us |
|---|---|
| The pharaoh of Egypt afflicts the Israelites and holds them captive. | Satan afflicts us and holds us captive in sin and darkness. |
| Moses leads the Israelites out of captivity through God's miraculous power, parts the Red Sea, and the people walk across dry land to a new life on the other side. | Jesus, our Savior, leads us out of sin by His miraculous power as we follow Him into the waters of baptism and rise into a new life of faith and freedom from Satan. |
| The people of Israel start to suffer. They miss Egypt. They doubt their prophet. They complain terribly, want to go back, and sin repeatedly. | As newly baptized Christians, we experience hard times, feel disoriented, and begin to doubt God's promises to us. We lose our vision of the promised land. Many of us return to our sinning. |

| God and the People of Israel | How This Relates to Us |
|---|---|
| **God enforces the boundary** defined by His commandments. He says in effect, "You went too far. I've been merciful toward you, but you repeatedly crossed the line with your unbelief and terrible deeds. You're not going to enter the promised land for forty years and until all those who sinned are dead." Why did God do it? Because, as their Father, He loved them and knew disaster lay ahead if they didn't live more righteously. | If we turn our backs on the grace of Christ and His newness of life, God chastens us with trials and challenges until our most sinful desires and habits are purged— because He loves us as a Father who chastens a child and wants him to prosper and live with Him in eternity. |
| God comforts and protects Israel through a cloud by day and pillar of fire by night even though they are still wandering. | God is always near and watching over us, no matter our situation or how imperfect we are. |
| After the evildoers among Israel have all passed away, God leads the remaining Israelites to the promised land with a commandment that they must kill the current inhabitants of the land (who were shockingly wicked)[2] and secure their borders, creating a land purely their own. **In other words, God is directing them to establish boundaries for physical and spiritual security.** | Even as God purges us "in the fire of affliction" to remove our sinful desires, he also expects us to establish clear spiritual boundaries with family, friends, and strangers alike, to let good things in but keep bad things out. |

| God and the People of Israel | How This Relates to Us |
|---|---|
| The Israelites do not establish strong boundaries but allow themselves to mingle with other cultures. They lose their identity, fall into wicked behavior, and are destroyed and scattered. | While we may not all hit rock bottom like the people of Israel, to a lesser extent, we experience misery and confusion when we do not hold true to our personal boundaries and faith in God. |
| God promises to gather and restore the people of Israel to the promised land before He comes again and invites them into the kingdom of heaven. | No matter the twists and turns in our lives, we have the same promise that God always reaches after us and will not stop seeking our safe passage into heaven. |

## Old Testament Lessons on Boundaries

Consider what we can learn about boundaries from the story of God's dealings with the people of Israel. As you read, compare what you learn to your own situation:

1. God set boundaries for His people in the form of commandments.
2. God was long-suffering and patient when they didn't obey, but when they "went too far," in His perfect judgment, He said in effect, "That's it. No more."
3. When God decided a boundary had been crossed and required enforcement, He said in effect, "Here's how it's going to be." He told His people what He was going to do and what He expected of them. (In this example, God forbade entry in the promised land. At other times, he allowed their enemies to win battles or even take them captive. God allowed unpleasant consequences to stir them up to a remembrance of Him and encourage deep reflection.)
4. When God's people were told to go into the promised land, He directed them to drive out the current inhabitants, whose values and behaviors were grossly wicked and out of line with God's standards.

5.  When God's people did not establish boundaries with neighboring peoples but allowed "foreign elements" to mix with their culture, they faced stiff consequences. They lost their identity as a godly people, experienced years of misery, and were ultimately destroyed and scattered. This is like the misery we experience when we allow our spouses and others to violate fundamental physical and psychological boundaries.

## Examples of Boundaries

So, what do spiritual boundaries look like?

*In the physical world, boundaries are easy to see. Fences, signs, walls, moats with alligators, manicured lawns and hedges are all physical boundaries. . . . In the spiritual world, boundaries are just as real but often harder to see.*[3]

Let's get specific about what boundaries in a marriage look like. To see how boundaries differentiate you and your spouse in three basic ways, take a look at the following questions and answers:

1.  **Who is responsible for what?** I am responsible for (this). You are responsible for (that). Do not try to make your responsibilities my responsibilities.
    - **Examples:** Your spouse is responsible to wake up on time for their job, control their tongue, develop their own faith in God, attend their own medical appointments if they are physically and mentally able, fulfill previous commitments made to you, eat right, take care of their body and hygiene, etc.
2.  **What will I not tolerate?** You cannot do (this and that) to me, or I will (such and such).
    - **Examples:** Bring drugs into the house. Spend money on porn. Disrespect you verbally. When your spouse says a certain outrageous thing to you, you may respond with, "That is totally disrespectful, and I don't want to hear that from you." Be prepared to de-escalate by temporarily stepping away or leaving the house and revisiting the topic when things are calmer.

3.  **What must I be permitted to do?** I need (this and that) to be healthy, safe, and close to God. You cannot prevent me from doing it, or I will (such and such).

    ▪ **Examples:** Quiet time after a certain hour or a safe, quiet space. A living space free of stench or filth. Access to transportation or essential finances. To attend church. Say prayers with our children.

This chart, inspired by the work of Cloud and Townsend,[4] illustrates more examples of boundaries.

| Boundary Example | How to Communicate/Enforce It |
|---|---|
| Words | Say no. <br> Say, "I like this" or "I don't like that." <br> Say, "I need this in order to (whatever)." <br> Say, "We agreed that (such and such) is your responsibility, not mine. I'm not doing it." |
| Truth/Integrity | Say, "I believe (such and such); therefore, it's important that I act like (this and that). I need you to respect that about me." |
| Geographical Distance | Move to a different room for a while. <br> Live in different homes for a time. <br> Formalize a legal separation agreement. <br> Get a restraining order to protect you from unwanted contact and abuse. |
| Time/Emotional Separation | Agree on a certain timeframe with no interaction (including text messages and calls) to allow for rest and reflection. <br> "Pull back" emotionally for a time, waiting for signals that it's safe to interact more openly and deeply again. For a while, keep communications focused on concrete activities, like the necessities of life, and avoid engaging over feelings and relationship issues. |

| Boundary Example | How to Communicate/Enforce It |
|---|---|
| Freedom to Interact with Others | Find appropriate people to talk to, including friends and professionals who know how to listen and keep things confidential. Join support groups (in person or online); hear their stories and share your own. Get active or stay active in church and participate in service, ministering, etc. |
| Plan Consequences | (Note: Failure to enforce consequences means you have no boundaries.) Think ahead about how you will act if the boundary is crossed. This can be complex and is never a perfect science. Have a plan B, C, D, etc., and enact it. Enforce your boundary by saying things like "We agreed to talk for ten minutes, after which I would leave. I have to leave now." Do it. Allow others to experience the painful, even tragic, consequences of their decisions. Do not enforce boundaries the way your parents or others may have enforced them with you: "Old-fashioned" parenting often resorted to beatings and yelling, as if those were effective ways to enforce boundaries. They are not effective. Be loving and listen to the Holy Spirit. |

## The Backlash of Enforcing Boundaries

*"If we walk away from risk to keep ourselves safe . . . we will waste our lives,"* said author and pastor John Piper.[5]

Taking the step to enforce a boundary is a risk, but it will prevent you from wasting your life in cycles of recurring misery. Most spouses with serious illness or addiction freak out when their spouse starts defining boundaries and enforcing consequences. For example:

**Backlash:** Your spouse may say you are threatening and manipulating them by issuing unfair, unkind ultimatums.

- **Remedy:** Don't let them change the lingo to make *you* seem like a manipulator torturing *them.* Remind them you have a responsibility to care for your most basic needs, you are not responsible for them, you are permitted to do certain essential things, and you have the right to not tolerate certain behaviors or living conditions. Tell them, "You have a responsibility to respect my needs." You will probably have to say this in various ways and many times over weeks or months, combined with consequences.

**Backlash:** Your spouse will probably say you are selfish, inconsiderate, and unsupportive because you know how many problems they have and are not being flexible.

- **Remedy:** Keep focusing on who is responsible for what and how you are not going to help them do things they can and should be doing for themselves. Assure them you want to help them through their problems but in a healthier way, as recommended by mental health professionals. Invite them to read about the importance of boundaries and to get professional help by making and keeping appointments.

**Backlash:** Your spouse may threaten you with various awful, frightening things, including harming themselves, taking your children away, posting all sorts of things on social media, and telling your family true or untrue things.

- **Remedy:** Do not retaliate or sink to their level. Stay loving, focused, and consistent. You want your relationship to improve. You know limits are necessary for yourself and for them. Tell them, "You are responsible for your actions. I'm just telling you what I need, and I need you to respect that."

As Cloud and Townsend have said,

> *You cannot change others. More people suffer from trying to change others than from any other sickness. And it is impossible. What you can do is influence others. But there is a trick. Since you cannot get*

*them to change, you must change yourself so that their destructive*
*patterns no longer work on you. Change your way of dealing with them;*
*they may be motivated to change if their old ways no longer work.*[6]

In the long run, your spouse will feel safer and happier after you
enforce boundaries because, in most cases, they subconsciously crave
order and control in their life. They just don't see the boundaries right
now because you haven't been clear enough or they lack boundary skills.

Like it or not, you are probably helping them form the boundary
skills they should have learned in childhood but for some reason did not.[7]

## Helen's Perspective

[How she would have felt years ago]: There is nothing, absolutely nothing
I hate more than when Christian walks away from me when I'm upset or
yelling at him. That's when I need him the most! He's supposed to love
me unconditionally. That's his job as my spouse. I feel so empty when he
shuts me out like that. The voices in my head and my anger go through
the roof, and all I can think of is how to make him stop going away from
me . . . or make him suffer because of how bad he is hurting me.

When Christian tells me no about anything important or even hints
at anything that could lead to a separation, I start thinking, *He doesn't*
*really love me. Nobody can ever love me. People always leave me.*
*They say they love me, but they don't.*

He started talking about boundaries, and all I could think was that
boundaries are for people who hate each other, like quarrelling neighbors
who build fences. Spouses are supposed to be close about everything.
I think he's just pushing me away because he doesn't love me and he's
probably found somebody else. He's getting ready to leave me.

[Fast-forward twenty-seven years]: Although boundaries still make
me nervous, I have come to understand how important they are both
for Christian and me. I had major boundary issues. What I expected
from my husband was impossible for any man to fulfill. I expected
him to make me happy and fulfill all my needs at all times, whether I
expressed them or not. He was supposed to say the right thing, at the
right time, in the right way, and if he didn't, he didn't love me enough.

That kind of thinking was so wrong. We now have a much better
understanding of what each of us needs, and I have learned to respect

his boundaries, which has helped me develop a healthier sense of self and my own boundary needs.

Just recently, I looked back on the times we lived apart. I was a lot calmer and, in some ways, happier. I now see that my obsession to expect my husband to show me perfect love all the time got me all worked up and triggered lots of fights. My learning how to find peace for myself, how to be me, and how to respect his boundaries finally helped us be at peace living together.

## Threats of Suicide

My wife frequently threatened suicide when I asserted my boundaries. At least twice, she tried to swallow large volumes of pills right in front of me—once when we were on a cruise ship supposedly having a good time. What a horrible ordeal!

When we were in process of separating, she would sometimes mention killing herself and get very, very detailed about what she was feeling and what she would do. It was beyond painful.

But I was not God. God was God.

Her choices were not mine to control. I knew I had to do certain things for my safety and recovery, and I had to leave her to whatever consequences came. I accepted that she might die. I hated it, but I had to steel myself against the fear of it.

These were soul-stretching times where I felt I was looking death in the face and dreading that I might have to live with the memory of a horrible suicide. But my conscience was clear, and with God's help and the perspective I gleaned from the scriptures, I knew Helen was responsible for Helen and I was responsible for myself.

If she chose to suffer, she would suffer. And if God would not heal her, then so be it, but I would take refuge in God. He never let me down in terms of being there.

## The Tight-Rope Walk

The acts of defining, communicating, and enforcing boundaries are definitely an art form. There's a learning curve for everyone, and nobody gets it right all the time.

Your loved one's behaviors are unpredictable. You've probably developed "antennae" that stick out of your head much of the time, trying to catch signals that help you monitor moods and states of mind, right? When you sense your spouse is "not in their right mind," you may wisely choose not to enforce something that's more of a strong *preference* than a firm *boundary.*

Photo by Casey Horner on Unsplash

Many times, my thought process went like this:

- If I enforce my need for (such and such) right now, my wife is going to have a meltdown, which could lead to intense fighting or hospitalization, which I can't deal with now because of (such and such; e.g., project at work, family event coming up).
- I'm going to gently remind her at a later time of my needs and our previous agreement to do (such and such), which may still result in a backlash, but so be it.
- Helen has shown progress in (such and such) areas, and I have to remember that life is often two steps forward and one step back. I will compliment her on things that are going better and show her my love.
- I'm praying for wisdom and guidance to know when to take a stand and when to be flexible.

## Gridlock versus Boundary Setting

Let's clear up a potential point of confusion: the distinction between boundaries and personal preferences, tastes, opinions, etc. You may recall this quote from chapter 4: "Can I Survive This?":

> *Most marital arguments cannot be resolved. Couples spend year after year trying to change each other's mind—but it can't be done. . . . Instead they need to live with it by honoring and respecting each other.*[8]

The above quote has to do with things that do not fundamentally violate you. In my driving-too-fast example, both spouses are hurt and upset about the other's views. But this is different than a spouse who threatens violence against you in front of your crying children, or a spouse who won't stop bringing alcohol into the house, or one who secretly plunged your family into another $10,000 worth of debt, or one who will not follow medical advice, attend appointments, etc.

## What Is Gridlock?

Gridlock occurs when you can't verbally come to an agreement about something you wish you could agree upon:

- You've had the same argument over and over.
- Neither of you can discuss it with humor or affection.
- Your differences seem to be greater and greater.
- And here's the kicker that can blur the line with boundaries: the thought of compromise makes you feel like you're selling out or giving up something that's part of your beliefs, values, or sense of self.[9]

The key to avoiding gridlock is surprisingly simple:

*When couples are able to treat their perpetual problems as they would a pesky allergy or bad back, they know the difficulty won't ever go away, but they manage to keep it from overwhelming their life together. . . . Remember that you don't have to solve the problem to get past gridlock. Neither of you has to "give in" or "lose." The goal is to be able to acknowledge and discuss the issue without hurting each other.*[10]

## How Boundaries Differ from Gridlock

When defining and communicating boundaries, your goal is to explain why you need to establish a certain boundary and how it will benefit you and your relationship. You may have tried to have a civil conversation about it but your spouse won't support what you know is critical to your well-being or theirs.

At some point, however, you decide the discussion phase is over and the enforcement begins. In effect, you say, "Here's what I'm going to do." And it doesn't matter whether they agree or not.

When enforcing boundaries, you simply inform your spouse of what you intend to do and briefly remind them of why you need to do it. Then, as described earlier, you manage any backlash.

You stay calm and in control. Gradually, your spouse begins to understand that there really *is* a moat with an alligator in it and they need to respect your boundary or the consequences will escalate.

If you don't eventually enforce a boundary, you have just removed the moat and totally disempowered yourself, fueling more chaos. On the other hand, once you experience an effective boundary enforcement, the next conversation about that boundary will look and feel vastly different, and your moat will be clearly visible to both parties.

## My Testimony to You

Setting boundaries is one of the hardest things you will have to do, but it's also what God does with us. It is right and it is necessary.

> ☀ If you don't define, communicate, and enforce your boundaries, you are hurting your relationship.

When the people of Israel went too far, God enforced significant consequences. When His people failed to establish boundaries with their neighboring nations, they ended up in dire straits, felt miserable, and were ultimately destroyed.

I promise you that if you will set and enforce boundaries with love and do your best to apply flexible judgment with the help of the Holy Spirit (not based on whims and bad moods), you will gradually see order and stability enter your relationship—or it will become clear that you must separate.

Your spouse will begin to know when you mean business, and he or she will begin to hate the pain when the two of you have conflict over the same boundary issues.

# Hope and Help

## Scriptures to Ponder

> *He that hath no rule over his own spirit is like a city that is broken down, and without walls. (Proverbs 25:28)*

> *Be not deceived; God is not mocked: for whatsoever a man soweth, that shall he also reap. (Galatians 6:7)*

> *No discipline is enjoyable while it is happening—it's painful! But afterward there will be a peaceful harvest of right living for those who are trained in this way. (Hebrews 12:11, NLT)*

## What You Can Do Today

- Read the Christian-oriented book, *Boundaries: When to Say Yes, How to Say No to Take Control of Your Life,* updated and expanded edition by Henry Cloud and John Townsend. It's life-altering. There are many detailed examples and recommendations about setting boundaries plus helpful Bible references.
- Think of one boundary (or more if you'd like) your spouse frequently crosses.
  - What is your spouse responsible for that they are not doing and trying to push off on you?
  - What is your spouse telling you to do or not to do that is fundamentally not okay with you and makes you feel like your identity is being robbed?
  - What is your spouse preventing you from doing that is critical to your own well-being and health?
  - What types of communications and behaviors from your spouse are violating you emotionally?
- Once you've identified the one boundary most important to you and hurts you most when crossed, take it to prayer and ask God specifically to help you identify a strategy to explain it to your

spouse and safely hold firm on that boundary. This could take days or weeks to carefully consider. Follow the inspiration. Remember these guidelines by boundaries experts:[11]

- First, figure out what you will gain by setting this boundary and compare it to what you stand to lose as you enforce it and deal with any resistance.
- Second, decide if you are willing to risk the loss.
- Third, go through with the plan as best you can, but anticipating your spouse's responses, also have a plan A, plan B, etc.
- Fourth and finally, realize that the hard part is just starting. The first time you enforce boundaries, you introduce a new dynamic into your relationship that often results in upheaval. It's not convenient, but it is worth it.

## Spiritual Blessings for You

Look forward to the wonderful blessings of patiently persevering with your spouse or loved one in partnership with God.

- Greater understanding of the character of God, including not giving in all the time or being a pushover when His children cross eternally important boundaries
- Greater clarity about who you are and what you need to feel well
- Greater self-confidence as you assert your needs while relying on God for strength and guidance
- More empathy for how God must feel when He sets boundaries and His children disregard them

## Chapter 9
# I Can't Plan Anything!

I cannot begin to count the number of times my wife insisted we break a commitment or change plans because she was angry, depressed, fearful, or simply didn't want to do something. As a person who strongly values following through and being consistent in word and deed, I hated this.

Sometimes I was the only one impacted. More often, our last-minute changes affected others who just shook their heads in disappointment. My parents experienced this a lot.

It seemed like the more important the commitment, the more likely it was to be cancelled or preceded by a hellish fight and the decision to go after all. Christmases, anniversaries, and birthdays were the worst.

And then there were the children.

Helen was always tremendously popular with children. She had an energy and a love for them to which they were magnetically drawn. They couldn't wait to spend time with her and loved being invited to our home or having us come over to "play." Helen actually sat on the floor and played with them. She was like no other adult they knew!

Imagine the heartbreak when I had to call their parents to say we couldn't come over after all or I had to face them in our home and say they would have to go home early and we had to stop the fun activity because Helen suddenly wasn't feeling well.

I was the "fun-sucker," the face of gloom, the bearer of sad tidings—over and over and over.

## Managing This Thing We Call Time

People seem to have widely varying skills when it comes to managing time, planning things, and getting things done. We all know people who are super organized and just seem to be more productive and reliable than others. I'm sort of in this category. Professionally, I'm a certified project manager, which means I'm supposed to be an expert at forecasting future events, figuring out how long it takes to do things, managing potential risks, making contingency plans, and keeping track of everything.

Oh, the irony.

But I learned to adapt, and I grew spiritually.

It took me decades to realize I needed to stop thinking of her as weak-willed when it came to changing plans. That was unfair of me and harmful to her.

Helen lives in a three-day span of reality. She can't stay connected to her past thoughts and plans or envision her future behavior beyond those three days. Commitments made too long ago don't factor into her current thinking. Anything that falls outside that three-day window becomes a flip of the coin as to whether it will happen. Calendars help, but not too much.

Other mental health disorders, such as obsessive-compulsive disorder (OCD), have a similar effect on a person's ability to plan and fulfill commitments. A person with OCD may spend hours and hours compulsively cleaning and organizing and have great difficulty breaking away, therefore often disappointing their spouses, missing important events, and losing their jobs.

## Making Time Your Friend (Jesus's Way)

So, what are we to do? I love my spouse, and because you're reading this book, I'm guessing you love yours. How do we keep living while frequently disappointing those around us (and ourselves) and yet thrive in this challenging situation? Here are some ideas that apply to all people but are extra important for spouses whose lives frequently change direction on a dime.

## 1. Schedule Events with Flexibility in Mind

If you're a committed planner and organizer, one of the things you like about scheduling things is that you gain a sense of control over your life. The murky future becomes less murky. You feel like you can reach far into it and shape it. Best of all, you feel like you can check things off the list with complete confidence that they will be handled properly and at the right time. Hands dusted, in the bank, all set.

But when you live with someone who struggles with fulfilling plans and keeping commitments, you lose that feeling of control. You are forced into a chaotic world that you would *never* tolerate independently. So now what? Do you stop scheduling and planning altogether?

No.

We recommend the following approach. Learn TPR:

- **T**hink flexibly.
- **P**lan flexibly.
- **R**oll gracefully with the changes.

**Thinking flexibly** means you stop taking your plans quite so literally. You think of your plans as penciled-in versus engraved in stone.

You can't take your plans to the bank and check them off the list anymore. They're a little more lively. They wiggle a little and may jump off the page. With every plan, your heart has to be ready to watch that plan change or be cancelled. This may break your heart and violate an extremely important value of yours. However, before you determine this utterly unacceptable, consider that flexible planning is not the same as complete chaos and the absence of planning—although it may feel that way at first. It just means plans are more like hopes and tentative arrangements. The future is still a bit murky.

**Planning flexibly** means you mentally run through a few backup plans. You routinely consider the impacts of having to cancel. This big shift in thinking makes planning more difficult and perhaps unpleasant. But it will bring a measure of peace if prior to making the plan you consider what else would have to change if the plan fell through. You ask yourself things like, "Which other person's heart might be broken by the change in plans? What financial impacts might there be? With whom will you need to communicate if the plans change?"

All of this may require you to divulge a bit more of your true marriage situation—and doing so appropriately is not always easy or comfortable. We recommend describing your situation in very "high-level" ways with work associates, community activity organizers, volunteering partners, etc. You might say, "We have some unique challenges in our family situation and require a bit of flexibility. Please know I'm fully committed to XYZ but can't always predict when my schedule will need to change." At least they know you have some challenges, broadly, and everyone understands the importance of family first.

**Rolling with the changes** means handling them with grace. It requires spiritual strength and a lot of maturity on your part to not blame your spouse—either in your heart or verbally to others. Much later in life, my family and friends grew used to the fact that Helen would not attend events or I would have to cancel altogether. I became much better at handling it in my heart and therefore could more effectively comfort others affected by it. If others sense you are angry and upset, it will feel like more of a big deal to them as well, and they may harbor resentment toward your spouse. You can do much to keep things calm and loving for all involved.

So how can you gain that ability to *grace*fully roll with the changes? How can you be at peace?

The remainder of this chapter presents powerful spiritual concepts that will help you move from despair at losing control over your life to the happiness found in the moment-by-moment trust in God He desires for all of us.

## 2. Live in the Present Moment

Jesus taught about living in the present and trusting that God will take care of things. Doing so is wonderfully stress-relieving. It can be hard at first, but learning to do this appears to be God's challenge, tailor-made for you. As stated simply in this updated translation of the Bible, Jesus taught,

*Do not worry about tomorrow, for tomorrow will worry about itself.*
*Each day has enough trouble of its own. (Matthew 6:34, NIV)*

I love the wisdom of that statement: "Each day has enough trouble of its own." What perspective!

As author Sarah Young captured it in the book *Jesus Calling:*[1]

*As you anticipate what is ahead of you . . . you are rehearsing your troubles many times, whereas you are meant to go through them only when they actually occur. Do not multiply your suffering in this way!*

## 3. Develop a Capacity for Mindfulness

The concept of mindfulness that has gained prominence in the West in recent decades draws from Buddhist teaching. Mindfulness is used today with great success in everything from medicine to mental health to corporate training and teaching stress relief to high school students.

Mindfulness is an important practice and skill that helps us learn how to live in the present with greater acceptance, nonjudgment, and compassion. As a child, we naturally lived in the present moment. But as we grew into adulthood, we were taught to think about our future and reflect on what we did in the past. We often escaped the painful present by daydreaming.

These behaviors gradually robbed us of our natural tendency toward living with an awareness and connection to the immediate, present moment.

If you are not familiar with mindfulness, please consider it imperative for you to study and practice. I encountered mindfulness as I began participating in yoga classes at a local YMCA during the darkest period of my life. Between yoga and mindfulness, my life was dramatically changed for the better. With Jesus Christ as the cornerstone of my life, these techniques comprised important beams and joists for my "house" to be built upon.

I read and reread a book provided to me by a therapist titled, *Calming Your Anxious Mind: How Mindfulness & Compassion Can Free You from Anxiety, Fear & Panic.*[2] Here are a few mindfulness techniques described therein:

- Feel every muscle and sensation of taste, smell, and sound as you close your eyes and eat a snack or take a drink. Feel it. Notice it as if you were an alien in a human body for the first time. Take no less than five minutes to do this. It may feel like an eternity but doing this will start to reconnect you with what it means to be "as a child" again in a very healthy way.
- Plant yourself in a comfortable chair or at the side of your bed. Feel the bed or chair pushing against your behind and hands. Feel the texture of the fabric. As thoughts of what you need to do today crowd your mind, gently let them pass without judgment or condemnation. Keep feeling and noticing and letting thoughts float away as they come to you. Do this for at least twenty minutes. Yes, twenty precious stress-relieving minutes.
- In a moment of fear or panic, focus on your physical surroundings. Don't push away the fear; just shift your focus to the appearance and design of the desk near you, or the squishiness of the car seat you are riding in, or the sound of the wind rushing past you as you walk to your next appointment.

Such practices will fully bring you back to what is real and present. This is an essential skill for anyone experiencing stress.

## 4. Trust God to Provide

As you strive to live in the present amid the change and chaos of your life, you will need greater trust that God will make things work for you—even when your plans are consistently blown apart.

> *Consider the lilies how they grow: they toil not, they spin not; and yet I say unto you, that Solomon in all his glory was not arrayed like one of these.*
>
> *If then God so clothe the grass, which is to day in the field, and to morrow is cast into the oven; how much more will he clothe you, O ye of little faith? . . .*
>
> *Your Father knoweth that ye have need of these things. (Luke 12:27, 28, 30)*

These aren't just pretty words. This is powerful truth.

God takes care of His own—the birds, the plants, and certainly His very children. He knows and He cares. We can learn to find peace amid uncertainty when we trust that God will direct our lives so that things work best within His eternally wise purposes.

## Recognize When God Changes Your Direction

At some point, for those dealing with a spouse who suffers from mental illness or substance abuse, the volatility begins to burn bridges with friends and family members. Not everyone will understand or be tolerant of the inconsistency—even if you try to explain it—and they'll begin to distance themselves from you. And then it hits you: this is going to change the course of our lives. And that may be true.

You end up with an inner conflict: "Do I stay true to my own values by honoring scheduled commitments, or do I prioritize my marriage, stand by my spouse, and learn to adapt?"

There's a wise saying attributed to Toby McKeehan and shared widely on social media: *"God will sometimes wreck your plans when he sees that your plans are about to wreck you."*

Maybe the lifestyle you hoped for would not have been as fruitful as the one God intends for you. In the Old Testament book of Proverbs, we read this important reminder of who's really in charge:

> *A man's heart deviseth his way: but the Lord*
> *directeth his steps. (Proverbs 16:9)*

There's a pearl of often-overlooked wisdom in this scripture. We may do our best to make plans, but God is the master of what truly happens in our lives. Certainly, our efforts matter, and God respects our well-intentioned planning, but we aren't calling the shots. He is. Sometimes our lives simply end up being very, very different than we expected or planned (see chapter 11: "My Hopes for My Life Are Unraveling").

### Helen's Perspective

[How she would have felt years ago]: I'm fearful when it comes to making plans. When a plan involves me having to do something or be responsible for an event, I don't like to talk about it. I avoid it. How many times do I hear I haven't followed through on what I've promised? Do I really need to hear it again? Christian wants me to sit down and make goals and plan events. I hate it every time he asks me, so I get mad, and then it stops.

But I do want things to look forward to. I feel like my life is so empty if we don't have trips and vacations planned. So I like talking about those because it gives me something to look forward to. I hate it when he doesn't think of those things himself. That's his job, isn't it? He's the planner. He should be planning fun stuff, too, not just things that have to get done.

I do love planning parties and fun things for kids, though they always seem to backfire because people don't do what I expect them to and I get mad and find a place to lie down or just say I can't do it anymore. But sometimes they work out really well and everyone says I'm really good at it. I like to make things fun for people.

[Fast-forward twenty-seven years]: To this day, planning is almost impossible for me. Most things get done at the last minute, or I have to cancel. Crafts get started, and some of them get done on time, but some don't. I just can't seem to be prepared and disciplined like some people. Oh, well. I'm more patient with myself now, and Christian is a lot more patient about that stuff too.

I love, love, LOVE organizing parties, but even today, I usually do all the work and get people excited about it, and then on the day of the party, I get so worked up I have to lie down and Christian has to tell people I'm not feeling well and won't come. That's really hard for me.

I think the biggest improvement we have made as a couple is that everything we plan is considered "sort of" planned. We know things may come up, and we tell our friends about it. So it's not as stressful anymore. It's just how our life operates. Maybe 60 percent of the time we follow through with plans, and 40 percent we don't. Christian seems to be okay with that and hardly ever gets upset about it anymore. I don't like hurting him, and it makes me feel better when he's not upset.

## A Godly Perspective on Patience

When we live with such uncertainty in our lives, one thing is certain. God is determined to teach us the virtue of patience. Patience is defined as *"the capacity to accept or tolerate delay, trouble, or suffering without getting angry or upset."*[3]

I like that definition a lot. It's simple and points to three things that challenge our patience:

1. Delay
2. Trouble
3. Suffering

Nobody wants to be angry or upset, but we do it to ourselves when we become impatient.

## A Mental Trick: Our Daily Twenty-Four-Hour Cube

Photo by Stephanie Pollio

It turns out there's a trick to learning patience, and we're going to share it with you. Fire up your most vivid imagination as you read this and you'll never forget it.

When you woke up this morning, your soul entered a cube we call a "day." It would be harsh to call it a prison cell. But, in a way, it is. Right now, you and I are in a twenty-four-hour cube more inescapable than the most secure lockdown facility in the world.

You walk into a brand-new, custom-made cube every morning when you awake. None is like the one you were in before.

Each day is made of a heavily frosted glass through which you can see vague shadows and lightened areas as you look forward.

Behind you, everything is crystal clear as you peer into the day cubes of your past. But you can only work, draw, eat, walk, run, play, hug someone, pray to God, or do anything else inside *today's* cube.

Pressing our faces to the front of the frosted, blurry glass to peek ahead does no good at all. It only wastes precious time within our "day." Nobody—not even H.G. Wells and his time machine—ever escaped their twenty-four-hour cube.

## God's Daily Lessons from On High

Now, envision a large opening at the top of your cube and realize that God allows good things, problems, and painful things into your cube.

You look over to your right and see someone shaking his fist at God.

You look to your left and see a man hiding from a problem in the corner of his cube, straining to see days long past that seemed easier.

Hour by hour, for the benefit of His children, God inserts an infinite variety of blessings and allows any number of problems to occur in the vast array of cubes spread across the face of the earth.

> 💡 We all have hopes for our future. We can all learn from our past. But we actually live in the present, which is hard to do when the present is painful. Do it anyway.

## Three Beliefs That Make It Easier to Be Patient

1.  Believe you can only do things today. Sound silly? Imagine the foolishness of standing with your face smooshed against the front of your cube most of the day or sitting tearfully crouched at the rear of your cube looking toward the good-old days instead of focusing on today while God keeps dropping blessings you ignore or challenges you run away from.
2.  Believe God will hand you good things through the hole in the top when it is in your best interest. You cannot and will not ever control what comes through that opening. And the challenging things will come to you when He wants to send them. It is always in your best interest to accept them humbly, including disruptions of your plans.
3.  Believe God is smarter than you are and knows what is best for you and your spouse. Stated like that, it sounds silly to disagree. But if we really believe it, why do we so often second-guess His decisions and timing?

Honestly believing and accepting these three facts makes it much easier to be patient with delay, trouble, and suffering because they expose the self-defeating games we play inside the God-given cubes we call "today."

And if tempted to fear the future, know that you will *not* be alone in that distant day-cube ahead of you. As Sarah Young wrote:

> *[When you] project yourself mentally into the next day, week, month, year, decade; and visualize yourself coping badly in those times, you are seeing is a false image because it doesn't include Me. . . . Say to yourself, "Jesus will be with me then and there. With His help, I can cope!"*[4]

# Hope and Help

## Scriptures to Ponder

> *The Lord is good unto them that wait for him, to the soul that seeketh him. It is good that a man should both hope and quietly wait for the salvation of the Lord. (Lamentations 3:25-26)*

> *And we know that all things work together for good to them that love God. (Romans 8:28)*

> *For I the Lord thy God will hold thy right hand, saying unto thee, "Fear not; I will help thee." (Isaiah 41:13)*

## What You Can Do Today

- If applicable, apologize to your spouse for not showing enough understanding for their changing needs and inner turmoil. Perhaps you have criticized them for being irresponsible or pushed them too hard. Mentally ill individuals crave for others to look compassionately past their irrational, difficult behavior and to understand that they don't mean to hurt others. It may be the last thing you feel like doing, but it is probably the first thing your spouse wants from you. This is a difficult topic because life goes on, children have appointments, work needs to get done, and you want to have a reliable spouse. Nevertheless, pray about how to find a balance between helping your spouse feel more understood and making progress toward adhering to plans.

- Face the tough reality that your life may not become stable and predictable for a long, long time, if ever, in this life. Remember the wisdom of the oft-quoted Serenity Prayer: *"God grant me the serenity to accept the things I cannot change, the courage to change the things I can, and the wisdom to know the difference."*[5] In most cases, your approach needs to shift from trying to change your spouse to accepting him or her and changing how you respond to the instability.

- Apply the twenty-four-hour-cube metaphor to your life by resisting the urge to mourn over your dwindling expectations of a perfect relationship versus smooshing your face toward the future and wondering when the problems will end. Prioritize learning patience, as defined in the scriptures and explained throughout this chapter.

- Try to imagine God smiling over you and know of His great love for the person you are. He believes in you SO much that He allowed you to have such grueling growth experiences. Feel it. Believe it. God really, really loves you. Thank Him for the MiracleGro®.

## Spiritual Blessings for You

Look forward to these wonderful blessings of patiently persevering with your spouse or loved one in partnership with God.

- More flexibility to go with the flow and gracefully accept sudden changes
- Greater peace within your twenty-four-hour cube, which is liberating and energizing, freeing you from the frustration of trying to do the impossible
- The gratitude of a spouse who feels more understood and accepted
- Greater insight into the mind and will of the Lord as you live within His plan for your day instead of trying to work around it or run away from it

## Chapter 10
# My Heart Breaks for My Spouse

You've probably seen movies where a prisoner is being harshly interrogated but stubbornly resists, saying "I'll never talk!"

Then they bring in the prisoner's wife or child. The interrogators describe the slow torture they will inflict on his beloved family member right in front of his eyes if he doesn't start cooperating.

The man's resistance evaporates. He hangs his head, knowing there's nothing he won't do to protect his family from harm and suffering—especially when inflicted right before his eyes.

It's heartrending to see our loved ones experience harm and suffering.

Many, many times over the years, I was left feeling aghast by what my wife was experiencing. I so often wished Jesus would instantly heal her. At times, we applied prayer, fasting, anointing with oil, the laying on of hands, and every faith-based means to alleviate our joint suffering. And while instant healing did not come, we made gradual progress.

In the meantime, I had to watch my wife endure the awful consequences of her illness. There were days at a time where she would lie in bed, unable to face other people or answer her phone.

Sometimes she would get so angry she would hit herself, rocking back and forth with her head in hands, sobbing in pathetic, hopeless tones, asking over and over, "Why doesn't anybody love me?" If I tried to counter her illogic, she would shriek "Stop hurting me!"

Several times she violently cut her hair with little regard for how she might look afterward.

After years of unstable behavior, some friends and even family backed away, telling me outright that they couldn't handle the drama or inconsistency. Some didn't say anything at all, but it was obvious they were staying clear of us. Helen was painfully aware of this.

Her physical disabilities got worse. She couldn't hold a job. She was less and less able to walk distances and even now is largely confined to her bed or wheelchair. We were also unable to have children—which was a slow, burning, ever-present agony for her.

What did all of this say about me as her spouse?

Faithless?

Helpless?

Worthless?

None of these things were true, but such painful thoughts did trouble me at times.

## What's a Spouse to Do?

Many times over the years, I asked myself, "What would Jesus do if He'd married Helen?" I wanted to follow His example. I wanted to act wisely in the face of tragic circumstances. I wanted to help without destroying myself in the process.

I tried to give her advice—often. I tried to get her to seek treatment and be more invested in her spiritual life and anything else I could think of to help her get out of her predicament.

Much of her behavior, however, was quite literally out of her control. It was the illness, not the beautiful woman and bride I knew was the real Helen.

I pleaded with God for understanding. I wanted to follow Jesus because His way is always best. But often, asking myself, "What would Jesus do?" yielded a big, empty, lingering question mark in my mind. He was never married (that we know of), and if He was, we don't read about His marital dilemmas.

The good news, however, was that my lack of understanding could be remedied by a more holistic view of the Bible.

## Jesus: God of the Old and New Testaments

*Disclaimer*: Before plunging into this section, let's be clear: the line between being fully accountable for rebelling against God and having a mental illness that diminishes a person's accountability is impossible for man to discern. That's one good reason God commands us to not judge/condemn others, including our spouses. When addiction enters the picture, it can be tempting to assume there is no illness at all and that your spouse doesn't love you or care. But we can't accurately judge. The scriptures that follow illustrate God's actions and feelings toward the Israelites whom *He* determined had willfully rebelled, which is not fully applicable to your spouse. However, we can still learn much that is applicable.

As we've seen in chapter 8, "My Spouse is Walking All Over Me," if we want insight about how to interact with our spouse as Jesus would, we should consider how God dealt with the people of the New and Old Testaments. Do you recall what Jesus said to the people of Jerusalem as He was about to be crucified?

> *O Jerusalem, Jerusalem, thou that killest the prophets, and stonest them which are sent unto thee, how often would I have gathered thy children together, even as a hen gathereth her chickens under her wings, and ye would not! (Matthew 23:37)*

Off and on for centuries, the people of Israel ignored God and misbehaved. Yet in these very words, we hear how the God of Israel wanted to love and protect them all the time, just as He was trying to do with the current inhabitants of Jerusalem while He stood among them in the flesh.

But He could not.

Even *God* could not help them—because they wouldn't let Him. So what did God do? He allowed them to experience very hard and unpleasant circumstances. But He always reminded them through His prophets that He was there, waiting with love and concern.

Here is an example of His love from the parable of the vineyard. After explaining the many good things God did for His people over the years and comparing them to a grapevine, God agonizes through the words of the prophet Isaiah:

> *What could have been done more to my vineyard, that I have not done in it? wherefore, when I looked that it should bring forth grapes, brought it forth wild grapes? (Isaiah 5:4)*

In this parable, the good grapes represent the wise, enlightened children of God who choose to rely on Him and therefore prosper and are happy. The wild, or bad, grapes represent children who choose darkness, are sinful, and end up unhappy. God is clearly agonizing over the tragedy of his temporarily "failed" vineyard.

> ☀ Even God feels sadness and yearns for His children's happiness when He sees them suffer—after doing all He can to help them.

But consider also that the story of God's people—and your spouse—isn't over yet. Things looked bleak, and the people of Israel were scattered and suffering. But change and growth can eventually come for God's people and for your spouse.

## Humbly Waiting on God

God respects our spouses' right to act for themselves and work through whatever experiences are necessary for their growth. He stands back and allows the suffering in our lives because it is part of His plan for us to learn humility, reliance on Him—and ultimately—Christlike behavior.

And He never leaves us comfortless. Even as we suffer, His message to us is this:

> The Lord thy God in the midst of thee is mighty; he will
> save, he will rejoice over thee with joy; he will rest in his love,
> he will joy over thee with singing. (Zephaniah 3:17)

See how God loves us? That love will be the thing that quiets you. He sings over you! Believe it. It is God's word to you. To truly feel these things in our hearts, we need to guard against incorrect messages from the world and even friends. Waiting on the Lord and trusting His plan for our lives is always wisest:

> It is better to trust in the Lord than to put confidence in man. (Psalm 118:8)

It's okay to rest within the refuge of God and to let His love quiet you as you picture Him singing over you, brightly, cheerfully, with encouragement.

Breathe. Pause. Soak this in.

Yes, God is our refuge.

## Who Knows the Source of the Behavior?

Our spouses sometimes act poorly, that's for sure. Naturally, we start to wonder which behaviors our spouses *can* control and when they are just being irresponsible and hurtful with their poor decisions.

If they are *willfully* irresponsible and hurtful, we are justified in addressing it, setting boundaries, etc. But what if their behaviors are due to their illness and truly out of their control? What if you know they should act responsibly but you're not sure they have the capacity to do it? They can certainly control some things, some of the time. But, wow, is it ever complicated to figure out where those lines are.

> It's often wisest to turn your spouse's care and discipline over to God and take care of yourself by simply taking refuge in Him.

## Long-Suffering and Slow to Anger

During one of God's many visits with Moses, He listed several of His godly attributes. These are, of course, Christlike attributes.

> *And the Lord passed by before him, and proclaimed, The Lord, The Lord God, merciful and gracious, longsuffering, and abundant in goodness and truth, keeping mercy for thousands, forgiving iniquity and transgression and sin, and that will by no means clear the guilty. (Exodus 34:6-7)*

The word *suffer* in certain older English contexts meant "permit" or "allow to happen." In other words, God is "long-suffering" when He is slow to anger and holds back judgment as His children make mistakes or act foolishly.

In other words, God allows us enough rope to hang ourselves—all the while trying to convince us to drop the rope! With God's help, you too can develop long-suffering and the wisdom of knowing when to stay silent and when to assert boundaries.

## Helen's Perspective

[How she would have felt years ago]: A lot of the time, when I'm upset, Christian could care less. I beg him to do what I want, and he just sits there and stares or tells me no. How is that loving? I don't ask for diamonds and lots of money. If I just want him to spend time with me when I'm really upset, he should.

Sometimes he tries to listen, but sometimes he won't listen at all, like I'm being bad or not making any sense. Don't you think I'm tired of being told I don't make any sense? The more I feel that way, the more I hear voices telling me I'm no good for him and I'm all of these awful things.

[Fast-forward twenty-seven years]: When I didn't think Christian was doing what I wanted him to do, I used to think he was just being insensitive and uncaring. But later I understood he was either protecting his emotional strength or trying to not escalate a bad situation. He often said I couldn't be satisfied no matter what he did. I came to understand that that was exactly true.

My needs and requests were so intense and ever-changing there was no way he could meet them all. So he was doing the right thing to take care of himself. Sometimes he would remind me of something I had learned in my treatment programs, though his doing so usually made me mad. But I realized he was not my "fixer" and I had to take care of myself using the skills I was being taught in therapy.

## A Comical Example: McDonald's Like Clockwork

Helen's eating habits were a serious challenge for her and of great concern to me because of their impact on her ability to walk, her overall health, and our finances.

Even though many things were unpredictable in my wife's life, there was a time when one thing was set in stone—a lunchtime trip to our local McDonald's—of which I was unaware until a certain chance encounter.

One day, my wife and I were walking through the hospital after a medical appointment when she lit up in recognition of a woman I didn't know.

"Hey, what are you doing here?" asked Helen.

"Oh, I'm getting some tests."

"Yeah, me too."

"Oh, that's right," the stranger said as if she'd known Helen for years. "Your surgery is coming up. Are your sisters still planning to come up and help?"

At this point, I was thinking, *Who on earth is this person that knows pretty much everything going on in our lives right now?*

After the conversation ended and we continued walking, I asked, "Do I know that person?"

Helen looked at me and chuckled with a guilty, toothy grin.

"I don't think so. That's the lady from the drive-through window at McDonald's."

Helen laughed at the stupefied look on my face. "But the dogs love going with me. You wouldn't want me to disappoint them."

Seriously? That's when I learned that Helen and our dogs piled into the car at 11:30 every day for a McDonald's lunch, where Helen had a daily chat with her "friend." This nice lady working at the drive-through knew more about our plans than I did!

What could I do? I laughed.

I love her. I really do. She still makes me laugh.

We discussed this McDonald's habit from time and time but, ultimately, I tried to stay clear of it. Yet I cannot count the number of times we donated bag after bag of perfectly good women's clothing to places like Goodwill and the Salvation Army because she couldn't fit into them anymore. It's tough to swallow when money is tight and you keep seeing fast-food bags and candy wrappers in the car and house.

During one four-year stretch where I traveled extensively for work, Helen was on her own to feed herself. Yet while I was away at work every week, nothing in the refrigerator ever seemed to move. I eventually learned that she subsisted purely on fast food and Peanut M&Ms.

All of this spelled trouble. Today, Helen's ability to walk is severely limited, largely due to weight gain and other complications. But of course, medications for bipolar individuals often cause unavoidable weight gain. So where did her responsibility for weight management come in, and what was simply out of her control?

We looked into stomach bypass surgery years ago, but they wouldn't approve it for individuals with certain mental health conditions because these people tended to return to their old habits.

The complexity of all this was too much for my limited mind. I learned wisdom when I stopped trying to figure it all out, focused on loving like Jesus, being long-suffering and slow to anger, and turned this aspect of our relationship over to God's care and discipline.

> *He that trusteth in his own heart is a fool: but whoso*
> *walketh wisely, he shall be delivered. (Proverbs 28:26)*

Note: The Hebrew word translated as "in his own heart" has a much richer meaning than our English word. It can also be rendered, "in himself," which suggests relying only on one's own mind, knowledge, thinking, etc.

## The Ideal Marriage

In the ideal marriage, both husband and wife continually repent and obey their Lord through the grace of Christ, each striving to love the other with the same compassion and tenderness Christ demonstrates toward us.

The result is a closeness and knowing of one another that can be achieved in no other way.

> *Everything in the [Bible] proclaims that marriage, next to our relationship*
> *with God, is the most profound relationship there is. And that is why,*
> *like knowing God Himself, coming to know and love your spouse is*
> *difficult and painful yet rewarding and wondrous. (Timothy Keller)[1]*

# Hope and Help

## Scriptures to Ponder

> *Blessed be God . . . who comforteth us in all our tribulation, that we*
> *may be able to comfort them which are in any trouble, by the comfort*
> *wherewith we ourselves are comforted of God. (2 Corinthians 1:3-4)*

*Humble yourselves therefore under the mighty hand of God,*
*that he may exalt you in due time: Casting all your care*
*upon him; for he careth for you. (1 Peter 5:6-7)*

*We glory in tribulations also: knowing that tribulation worketh patience;*
*and patience, experience; and experience, hope. (Romans 5:3-4)*

## What You Can Do Today

- While you are "waiting and watching" as hard things happen
  to you and your spouse, consider this recommendation from the
  spouse of a mentally ill person: *I made it a priority to keep my*
  *own emotional gas tank full. I believe it's important for those of*
  *us living with a spouse who has a mental illness to find things that*
  *fill us, encourage us, and make us want to move on and enjoy life.*
  *These may be leisure pursuits, a new career or volunteer work.*[2]
  - What can you do to keep your gas tank full? How can you take
    care of yourself without too severely rocking the apple cart at
    home?
- Remember the astonishing love of God the Father, who witnessed
  His Son suffer throughout His earthly life, including the
  unspeakable pains in the Garden of Gethsemane and on the cross.
  Remember that God knows what it is like to watch someone suffer
  despite Him doing all He can to administer relief.

## Spiritual Blessings for You

Look forward to these wonderful blessings of patiently persevering
with your spouse or loved one in partnership with God.

- More compassion for others, which is a primary outcome of
  suffering submissively before God
- Greater trust and deference to the wisdom of God and His
  purposes and timing for His children
- More gratitude for your own health and blessings
- Greater ability to discern the voice of God

# Chapter 11
# My Hopes for My Life
# are Unraveling

**A**s long as I can remember, I wanted to be married and treat my wife-to-be with great love and respect. Even as a child and young man, I recognized that women were the greatest, most precious of God's creations. I never understood or fed into the jokes my friends told about the stupidity of getting married or anything disrespectful toward women.

I loved the idea of two people sharing everything—their visions, their talents, fears, etc. I wanted to live that way more than anything, and I was certain that with my positive outlook on marriage, I wasn't going to experience some of the wretched things I had heard about.

Oh, the irony—again.

I envisioned being supported and encouraged to become my best self, doing great things with a loving companion at my side, and making her feel as loved as any woman on earth ever felt loved.

## The Last-Vacation Bubble

One year, shortly after the last of four separations, my wife and I went on a special vacation involving air travel and a car rental. I was super excited and sure it would be less stressful than our previous vacations-turned-nightmares.

That trip was the final nail in the coffin on my hopes that we could have a "normal" marriage where I was free to think and feel without having to anticipate and preempt her intense reactions to stress.

Our plane landed in Chicago. The air travel had been a little scary for Helen, the day had grown long, she was hot and hungry, and we were getting into our rental car when she noticed some minor scratches on the car. She curtly advised me to go back to the counter and get a different car so we wouldn't get charged for the damage.

I must have hesitated or said it wasn't necessary and she got angry. Like, *really* angry and lecturing me about not caring about her point of view and the legal and financial ramifications of not getting a different car.

The same old feelings and fears flooded over me. She was ready to completely snap, I could tell. My heart sank. Here was our special trip. I thought we could have some peace. Now this, again!

I went to the rental-car counter in an agitated state and ended up speaking to the same man who had helped me the first time.

Now, I like to be a positive guy. I like to lift people if I can. When this man helped me the first time, I could tell he was highly irritated about something. By the time we finished, however, he was smiling and much more relaxed. I smiled in satisfaction as I walked away.

But this time, I felt rushed because Helen was also mad about how long it was all taking. The man sensed my changed demeanor and seemed surprised that I insisted on a different car. He hastily made the changes, slapped the new paperwork together, and handed them over, looking annoyed as the line lengthened behind me.

I sighed in defeat. *I can't really be who I am,* I thought as I walked back to the car. *Look what's happened to me. I'm a mess.*

In the car, hours of dreadful silence dragged on, and one thought kept going through my mind: *I will never have a normal married life. I am never going to be able to just think and feel for myself without worrying about how Helen is doing, how she will react, and how to prevent this pain.*

That ended up being true. To this day, I must carefully monitor my thoughts and her moods and behavior. I frequently have to adjust my words and actions. Sometimes I wonder whether I am losing a truly foundational part of who I really am. Or, am I simply being more wise and developing better relationship management skills? It can be hard to tell. But this I know: God has given me peace in Him and far greater peace with my spouse. Ultimately, I trust that God is leading us for His eternally wise purposes.

We do not have what most psychologists would consider a normal marriage, although the tent of "what is normal" is pretty big and loose. Over time, we had to figure out a new normal. And I had to improve my coping skills and not sink into a victim mentality, while brooding over my squashed dreams.

I did learn. I have grown. I can now face major disappointments with great inner peace and composure.

## Deeply Held Dreams

Marriage researchers Gottman and Silver found that deeply held but squashed dreams (such as mine in the story above) are at the heart of many conflicts and create a great deal of stress for spouses:

> *Dreams can operate at many different levels. Some are very practical (such as wanting to achieve a certain amount of savings), but others are profound. . . .*

> *Our deepest dreams are frequently rooted in our childhood. You may long to re-create some of your warmest memories of family life from your youth— such as having dinner together every night . . . or you may resist having family dinners if the evening meal in your childhood home was often the setting for hostility between your parents that left you with indigestion.[1]*

Here's a partial list of Gottman and Silver's examples of deeply held dreams that spouses may not even be aware they long for. Take a close look and see if you recognize yourself in some of these. These are not obvious. Often, we don't even know we hold these dreams.

- A sense of freedom
- Feeling at peace
- A spiritual journey or lifestyle
- Exploring a creative side of myself
- Having a sense of power or winning
- Having a sense of order
- Being productive

## When It *Appears* Our Spouse Is Squashing Our Dreams

When we perceive our spouses are interfering with the fulfillment of our dreams, the pain and confusion can become intense. We may perceive that the only adjustment possible is to force our spouse to change or leave the marriage.

Long after the rental-car incident, I discovered that my despair that day had partly to do with a sense that my deeply held dream had been crushed: freedom to be spontaneous and be helpful with other people.

All I knew was that in one moment, I was able to take the time to be kind and uplifting to the man behind the counter and the next, I was the rushed, irritated person too fearful of my wife to be nice anymore. I resented having my identity and intentions jerked around like that.

The truth is, my wife didn't *make* me act or even feel that way. At that point in my life, I hadn't developed the skills to stay peaceful and allow my feelings to flow when experiencing stress.

Over time, I embraced a more empowered view of my life.

Because of my love for my wife and my conscious choice to stay married, I decided that I would focus more energy on her needs and emotional state, which meant I wouldn't have the emotional or mental energy to be as freely or consistently available to others. That's not being pessimistic or blaming her. It's just a realistic acknowledgement that I have limitations on my energy and time.

I could foresee the implications, and I didn't like it. But I was willing to accept it as a conscious choice, not because I was a victim. My friends would expect me to be consistent from moment to moment or day to day. What if they called on me for help and my wife wasn't in a good mood? Would I have to say no or cancel a previously made commitment, appearing to not care about them? Quite probably, yes. And I certainly would not be able to explain why I changed plans without making my spouse appear to be "the bad guy." So I would have to commit to helping others less often and be prepared for myriad unexpected situations that would require nimble responses that prioritized needs at our home first.

How can we find peace when it feels like our spouse is "pulling the rug out" from under our dreams, especially if our dreams include gospel-centered ideals?

## Helen's Perspective

[How she would have felt years ago]: We never should have gotten married. I know I'm ruining his life. I knew I would. I tried to warn him. Honestly, I just want to die so he can find someone else and actually be happy. He can't do anything he really wants because of me. He could do so much more without me.

When I feel better, I'm glad we're together and I beg him to never leave me.

[Fast-forward twenty-seven years]: I wish I could say otherwise, but I often still feel like I've ruined Christian's life. On good days, I believe God has given us our various challenges because He cares and knows that we grow and become more humble through life's hardships.

Christian and I often talk about what we have learned, and he tells me he has no regrets. I believe him, mostly. We are more mature now, that is true. We have relied on God to find peace and direction. And we both believe the only thing that really matters is our faith and how we act on our faith so we can live in joy with God forever.

I just keep remembering that this life is temporary, and I love how Christian has such a strong focus on what matters most. I know he really loves me. We have a wonderful marriage when I think about our lives in terms of eternity and what really matters. No marriage is easy, and these last years have not been all that stressful. I think maybe even less stressful than a lot of other marriages.

## Failing to Enter the Promised Land

When God first led Moses and the children of Israel out of Egypt, things looked rosy. They were out of slavery with a new life ahead, led by a God who could obviously do anything!

But Moses didn't know what lay ahead.

Moses didn't realize that the hundreds of thousands of people following him could be so immature, unbelieving, unwise, ungrateful, critical, disobedient, and stuck on their old habits.

Apart from God's wonderful miracles, the flight from Egypt ended up being a horrific disaster, with one incredible misbehavior after another.

You may recall that after a long period of disobedience, God finally decreed that His children would not enter the lovely promised land intended for them; they would experience this instead:

*Surely they shall not see the land which I swore unto their*
*fathers, neither shall any of them that provoked me see it.*

*... Your children shall wander in the wilderness forty years ... until*
*your carcasses be wasted in the wilderness. (Numbers 14: 23, 33)*

Ouch.

Imagine Moses sharing that memo with the elders at the next
morning's huddle: "Pass it out, men. That's the plan going forward."

## Wandering in the Desert

You've been handed a similar memo, but it's not all bad. There is a
valuable opportunity in this for you and your spouse.

I recall God frequently whispering three important messages to me
through the Holy Spirit:

1.  In contrast to the Israelites, you are not being punished because
    you've been "bad."
2.  Your mental health conditions will not go away suddenlyor possibly
    ever, in this life. The conditions are here to stay, but that does not
    mean either of you isn't trying hard enough or lacks faith. God can
    lighten your burdens over time, even if He does not remove them.
3.  "I [God] intend to form in you a high, even godly, standard of
    thought and behavior, as the scriptures teach: 'He that saith he
    abideth in him ought himself also so to walk, even as he walked'"
    (1 John 2:6).

I sensed that God fully intended to use our wilderness experience
to increase our Christlike-ness. He was dead serious about it, and I
needed to embrace it or suffer the consequences of "kick[ing] against
the pricks" (Acts 9:5).

In terms of this wilderness analogy, I perceived that the "killing
off of the wicked Israelites" was like God pruning and refining me by
killing off my sinful and ineffective thoughts, words, and actions. If
I acted sinfully or ineffectively, my suffering was greater. As I drew
nearer to Christ, sought strength in Him, and learned to love as He
loved, my suffering decreased and my joy increased. Over time, I sensed
that my inner "wicked elements" were being killed off.

These impressions gave me the fortitude to withstand my doubts as well as the voices of those who said, "You shouldn't have to live like this." In contrast, God was saying, "Trust and accept that I have designed that you live like this for my eternal purposes in your lives and for blessing the lives of others. You have wisely protected yourself [meaning, through boundaries] and your quality of life is steadily improving."

I have seen these purposes come to pass literally and perfectly.

## God's Support in the Wilderness

The new normal for the people of Israel was to forget about the land of milk and honey and learn how to live at peace with God and each other in this unknown, unanticipated wilderness.

But God didn't leave the Israelites to their misery, scratching in the dirt to eat bugs and dying weeds. It was surely a time of spiritual chastisement and discipline, but here's how He gloriously provided for them:

1. They received manna (bread) from heaven six days a week; on the sixth day, there was enough for two days so they could rest one day. (See Exodus 16)
2. God quenched their thirst through the miracle of water pouring out of the rock. (See Numbers 20:6–11)
3. God was with them through the cloud and pillar of fire. (See Exodus 13:21–22)
4. They had a prophet who provided guidance he received from the Lord, "face to face, as one speaks to a friend." (See Exodus 33:11, NIV)
5. They had a tabernacle and prescribed ceremonies to help them focus on God and learn His ways, including the scapegoat ritual, which was symbolic of the sacrifice and Atonement of Jesus Christ to enable forgiveness and new beginnings. (See Leviticus 16:1–34)

It's worth noting that people who had been trying to do their best to be obedient also suffered. Think of Moses, Joshua, Caleb, and the countless righteous women unnamed in the Bible but surely present.

💡 Your marriage may include years of "wandering in the wilderness," but God has not left you alone. The promised

> land is still the goal, even if you enter it a bit more haggard and battle-scarred than you would have liked.

Helen and I believe we have entered the promised land of our relationship—although it's very different than what I initially envisioned. We find great joy in many things and interact as friends on this God-given journey of life.

We enjoy a far greater quality of love than we could have ever imagined in the face of the "mental illness interference" that still gets in the way quite severely now and then.

## God's Loving Support in the Wilderness of Affliction

For now, you may have to consciously set aside some of your dreams, and that may feel like peering into the promised land but not being allowed to enter it.

Let's compare your delay to the "wandering in the wilderness" story in the Bible. God did not leave Israel without the great blessings described in the following chart. For each item, consider how God is working on your development (as opposed to simply granting your longed-for dreams).

| Wilderness Wandering | How This Applies to Your Marriage |
| --- | --- |
| The children of Israel were disappointed over not entering the promised land. | Assuming you know that your marriage is right, and you are committed to giving your 100 percent, you may as well accept the fact that your hopes for the ideal relationship are probably not going to happen in this life. <br><br> Your new normal includes a healthy acceptance that some of your personal dreams and hopes for an ideal marriage need to be put aside and that you, with God's help, need to prepare for some years in the desert. |

| Wilderness Wandering | How This Applies to Your Marriage |
|---|---|
| They received manna, and water from a rock. | You have access to the word of God through the scriptures and the Holy Spirit directly communicating to your soul. You have direct access to Jesus Christ. It wasn't coincidence that Jesus described Himself as the Bread of Life and the Living Water. God is schooling you just as He schooled the Israelites. He is training you to focus on Him for your daily sustenance instead of kicking back and living "the easy life" in a "land flowing with milk and honey." |
| God was with them through a cloud by day and pillar of fire by night. | The cloud and pillar and fire represent God's reassurance and constant, faithful presence protecting you from harm. Your awareness of this is heightened through your faith, trust, praise, and gratitude. Remember that unbelief was one of the major causes of the Israelites not entering the promised land. Believe. Believe. Believe in God. |
| Moses, a prophet, was their constant guide. | We have inspired leaders and caring ministers to provide counsel today. Also, remember that Jesus Christ is described as the great High Priest who intercedes for us with God. He is the true Messiah and the Great Intercessor you can access directly through your faith. (See Hebrews 4:14–16) |

| Wilderness Wandering | How This Applies to Your Marriage |
|---|---|
| God provided a tabernacle and inspired ceremonies and commanded them to participate. | We have resources available to us today, like our church family, ordinances like baptism and the sacrament of the Lord's Supper, gospel-study groups, family study, and more.<br><br>To not utilize these and go it alone is unwise. I testify of the importance of participating in your church family as you grow and support each other.<br><br>(In the days of Moses, can you imagine one family walking away from the whole company of Israel and heading solo into the desert? Dangerous! If you are living in your wilderness alone, you have separated yourself from resources vital to your spiritual survival.) |

If you consider the wilderness story to be an unfair and harsh analogy because you feel you've done nothing to deserve this pain in your marriage, remember the righteous ones among the people of Israel who also endured the forty years of wandering.

Consider these three clichés:

*We're all in this together.* (It doesn't matter who "caused" this.)

*God knows best.* (His plans are often unclear to us.)

*All's well that ends well.* (Short-term pain is worth long-term gain.)

## GREAT Relationships

Most Christians strive to live according to the teachings of Jesus—and that encompasses a lot. Our spouses may not take this commitment as seriously as we do, or they may not be able to apply themselves as fully as we do.

It's true that some things are just right and some things are just wrong. But we step into unhealthy territory when we think, *I'm right and you're wrong.* Before we know it, we are finger-pointing, judging, and being condescending—and Jesus taught that those are not right.

So how do we manage to hold to our conviction to live a Christian lifestyle—with eternity at stake? This isn't a matter of one spouse driving too fast or spending too much money.

In *Key Core Beliefs*, authors Otis, Williams, and Messina present a practical model for how to get along with your spouse while making progress toward the kind of life you envision.

The chart below is based on solid research and years of clinical experience in helping people achieve healthier relationships. These GREAT ways of thinking and communicating enable spouses to hold to their vision of what is right and what is ideal while respecting their spouse's views.[2]

As you read, compare your own thoughts and behaviors.

| Letter | Description |
|--------|-------------|
| G | **Genuine.** To what degree am I honest, sincere, open, and reliable? Can my spouse completely trust me and be at ease? |
| R | **Respectful.** To what degree do I honor the right of my spouse to make their own choices and be responsible for their decisions, even when I disagree? |
| E | **Empathetic.** To what degree do I care about my spouse and really listen to them, striving to understand their emotions, fears, and desires? |
| A | **Accepting.** To what degree do I accept my spouse as they are, without imposing my expectations, values, judgments, or criticisms, even if I disagree with them? |
| T | **Trusting.** To what degree do I believe in the good-hearted intentions of others by appreciating the best about them? |

If you're married to a spouse who doesn't take the gospel of Jesus Christ seriously, you might read these GREAT attributes and think, *That's not possible for a Christian who really believes in living the gospel in their home. Some things are simply right, and some are not. How can I respect or have empathy or accept the kinds of things I'm exposed to?*

We encourage you to pray about this model and seek the Lord's confirmation that these inspired questions are designed to improve human relationships. "Accepting" may be the hardest attribute to acquire. You will need the Spirit of God to guide your thoughts. You can still act according to what you believe is right, but your struggling spouse likely craves each of these qualities from you: genuine, respectful, empathetic, accepting, and trusting.

You can gain discernment from God on when it is appropriate to accept your spouse as a *person* and when to hold firm to your boundaries when their *behaviors* are not acceptable. There will be many things you can accept, perhaps far more than you've previously considered.

## Productive Self-Talk

Here are some examples that may help you define the new normal for your wilderness years together:

| Harmful View | Productive View |
|---|---|
| My spouse should be doing (such and such positive things), and it frustrates me when he or she doesn't. | I'm committed to doing (such and such) in my own life, and I'm working hard to figure out how to love, lead, and invite my spouse to do the same, like Jesus did. |
| My life is lousy because we're not doing (such and such). | My hopes for an ideal family life are not being fulfilled right now, that's true, but if I am a GREAT partner, we can eventually develop a new ideal, a new normal, together. |
| My hopes for my accomplishments and lifestyle will never happen because of my spouse. | It's not productive to blame my spouse. God has orchestrated the events in my life to help me become more like Him. I have the right to pursue dreams that will bring me happiness, and I have the |

> right to communicate those dreams to my spouse, but I need to balance my wishes with God's purposes for us. God will make more out of our lives than we ever could alone.

## Fast-Forward the Future

As illustrated by the rental-car incident, I was not able to live and think with the kind of freedom and security I'd hoped for when we first married.

However, as Helen's condition stabilized over the years, I was able to increasingly participate in activities outside the house and act more spontaneously with more peace of mind than back in those early years, thus moving nicely toward my vision for my life.

> 💡 Our new normal evolved in positive ways I could have never foreseen or developed without my wife's influence, desires, and personality.

I attribute these blessings to living according to God's word as well as becoming more skilled at interacting in GREAT ways with genuine, respectful, empathetic, accepting, and trusting thoughts and words.

# Hope and Help

## Scriptures to Ponder

*Weeping may endure for a night, but joy cometh in the morning. (Psalm 30:5)*

*And though the Lord give you the bread of adversity, and the water of affliction, yet shall not thy teachers be removed into a corner any more, but thine eyes shall see thy teachers [meaning we will see our afflictions as instructors shaping our souls]: And thine ears shall hear a word behind thee, saying, This is the way, walk ye in it, when ye turn to the right hand, and when ye turn to the left. (Isaiah 30:20-21)*

*"But my servant Caleb, because he . . . hath followed me fully, him will I bring into [the promised land] and his seed shall possess it." (Numbers 14:24)*

## What You Can Do Today

- Find a blank sheet of paper and draw a simple T-chart as shown below. This will not be a quick, easy activity, but it will be insightful and worth it.
    - Review the examples of deeply held dreams described in this chapter from Gottman and Silver's *The Seven Principles for Making Marriage Work.*

| My Early Hopes and Dreams for My Life and Marriage | My New, God-inspired Vision of My Life and Marriage |
|---|---|
|  |  |

- Pray for guidance that you will understand God's purposes for you and your family, including your spiritual growth.
    - Write your impressions of what your new normal might realistically look like compared to your early dreams.

## Spiritual Blessings for You

Look forward to these wonderful blessings of patiently persevering with your spouse or loved one in partnership with God.

- Greater understanding of the character of Christ, who suffered terribly because of the behaviors of others
- Deeper faith in God that your wilderness will, in fact, lead to a land of spiritual milk and honey, though in a way different from what you've envisioned
- Greater ability to hold to your integrity while communicating with others with grace, sensitivity, and nonjudgmental language

## Chapter 12

# Joyful After All

In this final chapter, we tie everything together with:

1. A brief recap of prior chapters
2. A warning about fear and techniques for managing it
3. An analogy of the surprisingly positive nature of "surrender to God," which is sometimes thought of as a painful requirement of only the most saintly, self-afflicting souls

## Concepts and Behaviors that Promote Healing and Joy

There's value in sitting back to celebrate your learnings by revisiting how you can work with God's plans for your life instead of chafing against them. What inspiration has God whispered as you've read these chapters?

### Chapter 1: I'm So Confused

- Spouses in effective marriages find ways to address all three dimensions of their relationship: 1) typical male/female needs and wants in a marriage, 2) needs driven by mental health issues, and, 3) sin and selfishness.
- Only God fully understands what is going on in your relationship and what it can become in the future.

## Chapter 2: How Can I Start Feeling Like Myself Again?

- Feelings are okay. Once they start flowing, they should not be suppressed. Feel them, then let them flow out of you.
- The effects of suppressing our emotions are so damaging that doing so can be considered self-abuse.
- At the root of all emotions are the AGRUP feelings: accused, guilty, rejected, unloved, powerless. An awareness of these can help you heal and manage future emotional flare-ups.

## Chapter 3: I'm Starting to Doubt Myself and My Faith

- Suffering with mental, emotional, or addictive issues can feel like wearing a deep-sea diver's helmet with defective eye, ear, and mouth pieces. These distort reality, making communication more difficult.
- Because it can alter our own perception of reality, we must learn when to stop communicating with our spouse when communicating becomes fruitless.
- It's not uncommon to begin doubting that God is good or is even there, but we can nurture our faith to a better place.

## Chapter 4: Can I Survive This?

- God will give you an answer to the complex question, "Should I stay in this marriage?"
- In most cases, the answer will be to stay, but abuse and illegal activities and God's foreknowledge of what our spouse will or will not do may prompt us to leave, at least temporarily.
- Fundamentally, marriage is about commitment. As the marriage triangle shows, when we commit to follow God *first*, we actually get closer to our spouse.

## Chapter 5: It's Not Fair

- Your marriage is not going to be fair. No marriage is completely fair, not even the "normal" marriage.

- God uses unfairness to teach us many virtues, as he did for many of the heroes in scripture, like Joseph and David.
- Focusing on the joy of doing good—like Jesus did—helps us endure severe pain and unfairness.

## Chapter 6: My Needs Are Not Being Met

- Meeting our spouse's "typical" male or female needs and wants can help prevent conflict and create a more satisfying relationship.
- We all want to be loved, but people prefer to receive love in different ways. Learning the five love languages can be a positive, eye-opening experience and help meet mutual needs.
- Like our devotion to God, marriage is a 100 percent commitment to our spouse, not 50 or 110 percent, regardless of how much our spouse is contributing (which we cannot accurately assess anyway).

## Chapter 7: I'm Totally Drained and Afraid

- Like the gifts Abigail presented to the mistreated, worn-out David, Jesus comes humbly before us, kneeling, as it were, and offering us the grace, love, and understanding we have not received from our spouse.
- We need our "love tank" to be filled by God so we have the love and strength needed to love our challenging spouses.
- We tend to look to sources other than God to find relief and comfort, but it is far wiser to look first to our God for these things.

## Chapter 8: My Spouse Is Walking All Over Me!

- You have the right and responsibility to define and enforce boundaries to protect your safety and overall wellness.
- God enforces boundaries with us all the time.
- We can and must risk establishing our boundaries, or we may end up dooming our marriage out of sheer exhaustion.
- Not all disagreements require a firm boundary. All marriages experience gridlock regarding nonessential preferences, which, though we may never completely resolve, we can learn to manage.

### Chapter 9: I Can't Plan Anything

- We must learn to live in peace within the unpredictable nature of our lives and create contingency plans.
- Staying within our "twenty-four-hour cube" helps us accept what God gives us in the present moment, not just wish for the past or dread the future.
- One of the blessings of our challenging marriage is that we will learn true patience.

### Chapter 10: My Heart Breaks for My Spouse

- Hearing God's own words of sorrow in the Old and New Testaments teaches us that we cannot control, fix, or make our spouses happy. Sometimes they must suffer as a result of their poor decisions.
- Focusing on what we *can* do is empowering and liberating.
- God wants us to develop Christlike attributes, like being long-suffering, slow to anger, kind, and to encourage our spouses (but never manipulate or control them).

### Chapter 11: My Hopes for My Life Are Unraveling

- Everyone has deeply held dreams of what they hope their lives and marriages will be like, almost like a "promised land."
- Like the ancient Israelites, you and your spouse are wandering in the wilderness instead of living in your hoped-for promised land.
- God provides many means of support and comfort even as we wander through our unexpectedly troubled marriages.
- Using the GREAT model of relationships (being genuine, respectful, empathetic, accepting, and trusting) helps us create a rock-solid foundation that can move us closer to the promised land.

## A Warning about Fear

You may have read much of this book with recurring thoughts like these ringing through your mind: *What if I can't do everything recommended? What if I'm still afraid of how my spouse may hurt me? What if my faith is weak and I don't feel close to God yet?*

Given all you have been through, your fears are understandable. Your future is uncertain. Your pains and confusion have been intense. The decisions you must make are constant and weighty. It is understandable that your fears lie at your doorstep and you are troubled by them.

But consider for a moment how such fears—if unchecked—can undermine your efforts. Rick Warren describes just three of the damaging effects of fear in interpersonal relationships:

> *Fear makes us defensive. When people point out weaknesses, we retaliate and defend ourselves.*
>
> *Fear keeps us distant. We don't let people get close to us. We withdraw. We hide our emotions.*
>
> *Fear makes us demanding. The more insecure we are, the more we attempt to control things. We try to have the last word in a relationship. We seek to dominate.*[1]

The Bible warns us to conquer fear. In fact, the counsel to "fear not" or "be not afraid" appears over one hundred times in the King James Version. It was a frequent commandment from the lips of Jesus, making it something we should take seriously.[2]

*Oh, great,* I've thought to myself at times. *So should I fear the fact that I am fearful because I fear I cannot stop the endless flow of my fears?*

God must smile with compassion when our fearful hearts take us on a self-defeating spin cycle like that.

If you're convinced fear is damaging and believe God must be serious about us conquering it, there's good news for you.

## Coping with Fear

Is the solution to notice each fear and drive it away? To chase it like a rodent or cockroach, which are sure to come back anyway?

No.

Throughout this book, you've read scriptures regarding trust, praise, and thankfulness. That's because a heart striving to trust, praise, and be thankful will not be as fearful or fearful at all. The light created by these attributes displaces fear. This is demonstrated over and over throughout scripture. (See Psalm 34:4; Proverbs 29:25; Psalm 56:3–4; Psalm 27:1–14; Psalm 115:11; Psalm 112:1)

When we focus on these positives, there's little room left for the negatives. The light of God that enters our souls naturally dispels the fear, meaning fewer and fewer rodents and bugs to chase. I testify that this works. Try it now.

Pick one of these right now:

1. Trust
2. Praise
3. Thankfulness

Talk to God with one of these attributes (trust, praise, or thankfulness) in your mind. Just sincerely say things like, "I trust you (or "thee," if you prefer), Heavenly Father." "How I love you, Lord Jesus! I praise you for coming to earth for me. Your example and teachings fill me with motivation and awe. I love who you are. I praise you. All glory to you and the Father. All glory and praise! As the scriptures teach, you are praiseworthy beyond my understanding." "Heavenly Father, I thank you for sending Jesus. I thank you for the people who help me. I thank you for the Holy Spirit, who is often near and comforts me. I thank you and praise you for (such and such other things in life)."

## What if you fear that you can't do what's recommended in this book?

- Your humble recognition that you don't yet have all these skills may be your biggest asset right now, your ticket to progress. Unwillingness to consider new things locks you out. Thank God for the inspired principles and recommendations found in the scriptures. They are building blocks.
- Start by *believing* what you've read here. You can choose to believe the biblical principles and psychology recommendations with the

hope that they can work for you over time. Praise God for inspiring professionals who research and then share what works with those of us who suffer.

- Identify the one recommendation that makes the most sense to you and gives you the most hope. Start doing it as best you can. Trust God that His word is sure and that His blessings will come.
- Every day, strive to trust, praise, and thank God.

## What if you have mental/emotional/addiction issues too?

- That's hard. You'll recall that I suffered with multiple diagnoses as well. Very few people are perfectly "normal." Focus on the recommendations that seem reasonable to you. Thank God for a talent or positive attribute that you have.
- Your willingness to acknowledge your issues is extremely healthy and a great asset. The reader who thinks they have everything figured out and would rather just change their spouse is the one who will likely continue to experience intense pain and cause more pain for their spouse. Praise God for giving you the awareness and humility to accept your condition.
- Despite your mental challenges, your spirit can still believe in God. Your spirit can still trust Him. Pray, "Glory to you, Heavenly Father, for your plan to help me become more like Jesus. I know your wisdom is greater than mine. I believe in Jesus, your Son, whom you sent to be a light and to save me. I believe. Help my unbelief as I humbly try." (See Mark 9:24)

## Hope from Those Who Have Been There

It's encouraging to read stories of those who have survived and grown personally through their frightening situations, like this perspective from a man named Russell:

> It really helps to view [my challenging situations] as opportunities for growth and personal education. Rather than see every conflict and tribulation as a crisis of unresolvable proportions . . . it becomes more about my choices than about my helplessness. And I can learn a lot from my choices.[3]

And here's a quote from Alex, a man who reflected on the blessings of his troubled relationships:

> *This was the greatest gift of being around people with*
> *[mental illness]: I got to see myself and how I interact with*
> *others. As painful as these relationships were, I needed*
> *them in order to become the person that I am today.*[4]

## *Surrender:* It's Not a Dirty Word

We end with a final perspective on experiencing joy, after all.

Key to experiencing joy in this life is working with God's plan for us instead of resisting it. In fact, that can be thought of as a simple definition of surrender in the spiritual sense.

The word *surrender* is not in the Bible. However, the concepts that constitute a spiritual surrender definitely are.

Most of us dislike the word *surrender*. We generally envision defeated, ragged, wounded soldiers coming out of hiding with their hands over their heads and waving the white flag. Who wants to be the first to give up? We're not quitters, are we?

No. We're not, and biblical spiritual surrender has nothing to do with quitting or abandoning the free will God has given to His children. A more suitable definition of *surrender* for our purpose is this:

> *To cease resistance or hiding from an enemy and submit to their authority.*[5]

This definition applies perfectly to life as well as war.

My wife and I recently discovered an amazing thing: a complete, original edition of the *Philadelphia Inquirer* newspaper announcing the end of World War II. We found it among my father-in-law's belongings just after he died.

There's an inspired message in this headline: PEACE.

There's biblical truth here as well because peace comes after surrender. Let's take a final look at how you can find peace even when life doesn't make sense in your unpredictable, painful situation.

Photo by R. Christian Bohlen

## Ending Our Trench Warfare with God

Picture everything described below as if you are there.

Imagine yourself in a deep trench like those of World War I. You decide to take a look at who is on the other side of the enemy line.

Peering over the top of the trench, about one hundred paces away, you see them. There, behind the enemy line stand God the Father and His Son, Jesus Christ.

What?

Well, yes. In this life, you and I have made God our Father and His Son our enemies (see Romans 8:7–8). Given our fallen nature, we routinely act contrary to God's will and commands. This is a scriptural fact.

Do you struggle with the commandment to forgive your spouse? Do you find it impossible? Does the resulting frustration create a distance, even an animosity between you and your Heavenly Father? Do you feel the complexity that surrounds your family situation is more than you can bear—even if you've read that God can help you somehow, somewhere, someday? Does your inner conflict and helplessness anger you? God is in charge of the universe. He sees all that happens to you. Yet it goes on.

So what do we do? Sadly, our weak, fallen selves fight against God.

When life becomes painful, we duck into our trench and try to hide our unbelieving, angry thoughts from God. Sometimes we boldly peek over our trench wall with an angry face, shaking a fist. We rise up and hurl angry accusations. We shoot arrows. We may even curse the blessings sent to us because they're not the blessings we wanted. We live as we please and not in the ways of light, truth, and obedience.

But then we open our Bibles and read of submission and humility.

*Submission! God is the one making life hard on me!* we grumble.

Photo by Richard Felix

At times, we may stop our rebellion, but our angry, confused hearts keep us tucked in our trenches, unwilling to stop hiding.

We then venture a peek over the top to see what God is up to. The Father and the Son are still there, smiling and waving. They gesture toward us. "Come out of there. Come over to us! We love you. It's better over here. Trust us and let go of this fight. We want to help you. We can help you. We love you and think of you all day long."

We sink back down, pondering this demonstration of love. But the trench has been our home for so long. And God has hurt us. He's made our life hard. It's not fair. It's *not!*

We suffer for months and then years, peeking over the top now and then because of beautiful promises in the scriptures. Sure enough, each time, we see Them waving and gesturing at us to come out and come over.

One day as you sit despondently, you decide to read the Bible. The Holy Spirit rises from the pages and softly enters your heart. You feel an unusual clarity and perceive this message: "Give up this pointless fight against the God who loves you so much. Stop hiding. Stop resisting. Submit to that authority who rules this universe. Submit to that wise and loving authority who created you and all other things."

You weep. "I want to," you say. "Okay, I see that my fight is foolish. Why do I fight against God and His Son who love me most? The rest of the world may fight against God, but I don't want to anymore. I'm ready. I do see."

You pop your head out fully now. They smile most heartily and with no resentment or judgment. Their gestures are eager and loving, greater than ever. But your feet are stuck. You just can't seem to get out. Your arm comes over the wall now, but that's as far as you can go. After a time of hanging on the edge of the trench wall, you sink down in despair as you recall your habitual mistrust and resentment.

"I can't. I can't really trust God."

Then more honestly, you admit the truth. "I don't want to trust God. I don't want to let go of my resentment and fear. I'm stuck in this hole forever. I know I should quit this silly fight, but I don't want to."

You sob in bitter silence.

\* \* \*

After some time, you hear something approaching above you.

In a final, feeble effort, you peer over just one more time. To your astonishment, you see Jesus Himself walking toward you, just twenty paces from you, striding confidently and smiling with encouragement.

You slide back down in shock. *This is unexpected*, you think. *He's coming all the way to me?* But then you remember the words of scripture:

> *I stand at the door, and knock: if any man hear my voice, and open the door, I will come in to him. (Revelation 3:20)*

The footsteps stop at the top of your trench. Jesus kneels and looks down over the edge. You look up with shame, yet a hint of hope. You remember the words of Paul:

> *For the good that I would, I do not: but the evil which I would not, that I do. (Romans 7:19)*

*So true*, you think. *I'm powerless to "surrender" even though I know it is good. God isn't forcing me. He's inviting me to leave this pathetic place and my foolish resistance and enter His presence.*

Mercifully, the Holy Spirit comes to you again and you hear His prompting: "Jesus will do what you cannot do, but you must do what you can, as little as that may be. Do it now. Do it."

You are frozen by the fear of change. But God has literally come to you from above, and now the Holy Spirit is speaking within you. Movement from above draws your eye.

You look.

Jesus is reaching down, His hand extended, waiting for you, the imprints of the spikes of the Crucifixion visible.

"Reach up and hold His hand," the Spirit prompts.

A surge of desire and conviction swells within.

"But how? HOW?"

The Holy Spirit answers, "Say 'I believe in you, Jesus, more than I believe in myself,' and mean it. Then raise your hand, as weak as you may feel. Picture placing your hand in His with childlike trust. That is all you need to do. Remember, Jesus saves you. You don't save yourself."

"I can do that. Yes, that much I can do." And you place your hand into the hand that was sacrificed for you.

Instantly, you feel the firm response as the Savior closes both of His hands around yours and you feel strength come to your feet. You don't know why, but your embarrassment over past wrongs evaporates.

Still holding on, you stand and breathe like you haven't breathed in years. You risk a glance into the eyes of He who has pulled you higher, and there is no condemnation, only pleasure and rejoicing at your decision.

*Why would I fight against a God who loves me like this?* you wonder.

With new courage, you say it aloud, with your head bowed before Him—not in shame but in reverence: "I choose to no longer hide. I choose to no longer resist. I get it! I finally get it! It's a good thing to do. It's the wise thing to do! I choose to submit to the authority of the one who is wiser than all and who loves me beyond my ability to understand. I choose to surrender."

Photo by Pete Will

After cresting the trench wall for the first time in your life and now feeling Jesus's arm around your shoulder, you see God the Father beaming with pleasure. The Great Mediator of all mankind has begun His precious work to bring you to the Father. The Holy Spirit burns within you, confirming the blessed decision you've made. You are heading home.

Jesus steps in front of you and turns to look you in the eye.

"There's still a battle ahead, but come, follow me," He says. "For the remainder of your life, watch me in real time as I walk just ahead of you. Keep your eyes fixed on me. If you study my life and remember my ways, the life you see in Me will become part of you."

You see it all so clearly now. Your challenging marriage is the purging, cleansing, searing fire that transforms you from a naturally selfish soul living in the dark trench of fallenness into a likeness of Christ, who continues to walk in front of you, enabling you and protecting you.

With the love and guidance of God the Father, the Son, and the Holy Ghost, you realize that you will be sustained and fed with whatever you need so *you* can be the person your spouse needs you to be while God helps your spouse in His own time and way, for your eternal joy, after all.

# Our Story

Helen and I met on the very first day that I became a traveling musician. My band was booked at a hotel in her New Jersey town for two weeks and we saw each other every day for fourteen unforgettable days.

Within days of meeting her, I sensed she had every quality I didn't have and more. I was completely in love and admired so many things about her even though we scarcely knew each other. To this day, people often describe Helen as a "light." She has an amazing energy, playfulness, humor, and sweetness about her. Everyone loves her.

I proposed marriage within a month of our meeting and I felt like the luckiest guy in the world when she enthusiastically accepted. Because the band traveled throughout Pennsylvania, New Jersey, New York, and West Virginia, we spent far less time together while dating than most couples. Nevertheless, we were married in less than six months from that amazing day we met.

As surprising and hard as our marriage turned out to be, I have no regrets. I believe God led me to her and we were meant to be. Great blessings have come to us and to many of our friends and family as a result of our union.

## The First Disagreement

I vividly remember our first disagreement. It was about two months after we met and my band was playing in her area again.

I was driving and she was a passenger as we navigated an area she knew well. At one point, she told me to take a certain exit. Just as I was approaching the exit, I said, "Wait a minute, are you sure this is the right one?"

She said nothing and turned her head away from me, staring out the window for the rest of the ride, completely shut down, barely acknowledging anything I said.

We were engaged to be married at this time, and I was totally confused. I grew more anxious by the minute. Then by the hour. Then by the day.

Three anguished days later, she came to see me with a little stuffed piggie wearing a sweater that read, "Hug Me." She apologized and was incredibly sweet, which I perceived to be her "true self" again. But what had happened? Why had she not returned my calls? Why this prolonged anger?

Little did I know that my questioning her about something she knew better than I did would put her over the edge emotionally.

I have an intense need to understand my surroundings and the logic behind decisions. I resist fully trusting others and want to comprehend things myself. To this day, this tendency of mine understandably conflicts with Helen's need to be validated and trusted (and it reveals issues of my own).

This was the first time I was stunned by Helen's instant and unrelenting anger. It was definitely not the last.

Three months after this episode and just before we were married, I clearly remember walking through a park as she tried to warn me not to marry her.

"I'm a witch, and I mean it," she said earnestly (and not in the occult sense of the word).

I laughed. Not this sweet woman. Sure, there had been a few stressful moments, I thought to myself, but with the light of the gospel, I was sure we could work through a few wrinkles.

She went on to say she had a lot of problems and didn't want to hurt me. I calmly assured her that everything would be fine, believing in my heart that our marriage was meant to be and that God would help us through it.

"Be ready to buy me ice cream when I'm mad," she said.

I was unfazed and remained certain that happiness was around the corner.

I ended up buying a lot of ice cream.

## Helen's Diagnoses

Helen has borderline personality disorder (BPD) and bipolar disorder, as diagnosed by several professionals. There was initially some debate whether someone with BPD could even have bipolar disorder, but experts now agree BPD is commonly combined with other issues, sometimes in clusters.

When a person's responses to stress consist of bewildering overreactions resulting in intense, long-lasting consequences, their condition may be considered "clinical" and require psychiatric diagnosis and treatment.

But as a young husband, how was I to know what was abnormal or typical of new marriages? I had heard marriage was hard. What I was experiencing certainly didn't seem normal, healthy, or fair, but I didn't suspect mental illness at first.

After terrible episodes that gradually escalated from prolonged silence, to angry words, to yelling, to Helen hitting herself, to nonsensical fears and terrible accusations against me and others, she would calm down and be as humble and kind and loving as anyone could imagine.

Sometimes she would instantly snap out of it and expect me to be perfectly happy and forget all about the problems. Over time, she resented my efforts to resolve or even understand what had just happened. She just wanted me to forget that anything had happened and snap back to normal like she had.

But I was whiplashed, hurting, and increasingly frightened.

## "Why Are You Punishing Me?"

Helen had almost no ability to cope with my feelings or reactions to her behavior. Neither of us realized it at the time, but I have bipolar disorder 2, a depressive version of the more widely known manic (hyperactive) bipolar disorder.

Because of my issues, when Helen had an episode, I would become stressed out, quiet, and depressed. She hated it when I wasn't happy or talking. She would cry, "Why are you punishing me?" over and over. I thought this was nonsense and told her so. I wasn't trying to punish her at all. I tried to explain I was hurt and shocked and exhausted by the painful episodes, but she seemed unable to comprehend that.

It was years before I learned that Helen's disorder caused her to regress to the mindset of a young child when under stress, which is a known BPD behavior. If I, as her husband (whom she subconsciously viewed as a parent), was emotionally unavailable due to stress of my own, she took it personally and interpreted it as punishment. She felt abandoned and neglected, as if she were a child locked in a house and left alone because she had been "bad."

The thought that her husband was an adult with feelings and needs of his own simply did not register. For nearly twenty years, it was incomprehensible to her no matter how I tried to explain it.

## Separations and Progress

Throughout our first year, there were never more than two weeks that passed without some kind of bizarre, emotionally intense blow-up resulting in her lying in bed and staring at nothing in particular. Usually, it was every two or three days.

After a year of intensely painful experiences, I decided to separate from her. I was praying about my decisions at that time in my life and felt it was best because I was near collapse.

After moving away and taking a short-term, menial job for a few months, I was blessed with the opportunity to use my education as a math teacher at the juvenile correctional facility I described in the Introduction.

I stayed in contact with Helen throughout the separation, and we decided to reunite. She joined me in the remote forest where the juvenile facility was located—six miles down a dirt road to the nearest tiny town, and thirty-five miles from the nearest McDonalds. This isolation didn't help her much because Helen is a very social person and she prefers the energy and excitement of a city.

At the juvenile facility, I worked with brutally disrespectful, dysfunctional young men for twelve intensely stressful years. It's impossible to describe the combined stress of dealing with them every day at work while being overwhelmed at home. I became deeply, severely depressed at times and began to lose touch with myself.

During this time, my wife and I separated two more times. The separations were helpful because I was able to ground myself again and set limits. I was being emotionally abused and I knew it, and it was not healthy to allow it to continue. With each separation, I could sense progress being made. Individuals with BPD, bipolar disorder, and addictions need to have clear limits or they can wreak terrible havoc in others' lives.

During one of these separations, I had filed for divorce. Filing for divorce triggered in Helen another fundamental fear common to those with BPD: the fear of abandonment. Psychologists consider this the number-one fear for many BPD sufferers.

The abandonment issue places the spouse or family member in a tough spot. They must set limits to protect themselves and help the BPD individual view their own actions from an adult perspective. But setting limits and separating from them triggers their spouse's darkest fears: "I'm unlovable. I will be abandoned, I know it," which leads to "I hate you" and "You never really loved me" statements.

Nevertheless, looking back, separating was the right thing and our relationship progressed.

## Medications

Back in our second year of marriage, I learned more about mental health issues and realized that Helen had some type of condition and needed care. She reluctantly began seeing a professional and was periodically in psychiatric hospitals during times of crisis.

Initially, none of the medications they gave her helped.

About ten years after we married, Helen was prescribed a medication that made a world of difference. Within days of first taking it, she walked up and looked right at me with such serene, hopeful eyes. "This is really helping me. I feel so much better," she said.

But medications have side effects, including weight gain. Because Helen's left leg is paralyzed from the knee down, she needed to watch out for weight gain, and so the years that followed were filled with trying different medications. Nevertheless, she continued to gain weight and that was concerning.

Around this time, her mother suddenly passed away, which was extremely hard on her. Soon after, her father began living with us.

Helen's overall mindset deteriorated, and no combination of medications or therapy seemed to help. At year fifteen of our marriage, there were still major emotional meltdowns about every three days, which was even harder to conceal with her father close at hand.

After a combination of bitter disputes, a miserably failed vacation, her new smoking habit which infuriated me, and discovery of her secret credit card that was nearly maxed out, I became despondent.

One day a voice inside me said, "That's it. You can't do this anymore." I just stared at the breakfast table and knew that was true.

I became resolute. I had given all I had to give at that point in my life. I was crumpling, and I felt the Holy Spirit sanction the decision to protect myself.

I told Helen we needed to separate and that I was going to file for divorce. This astonished both of us.

"How could this happen?" I agonized.

I knew our marriage was right. I had received so many witnesses from God! We had made progress in some ways. Yet I knew we were at a dead end and I had nothing left.

But God clearly approved the decision to separate and pursue the divorce.

## A Life-Altering Accident

We separated for the fourth time. At great inconvenience to everyone, Helen and her father moved into other houses, and I remained in Virginia, where I had taken a new job. I bought Helen a modest home in Pennsylvania, where I fully expected she would live the rest of her life with me supporting her, and I would move on as best I could. I had to sell our recently purchased, lovely house and I moved into a rental, the basement of a townhouse.

To this day, Helen painfully reminds me of how cold I was toward her on the day we moved her belongings into her new house. She had tried to joke with me and act like nothing was different. But I had resolved that the relationship was over and I was actively trying to emotionally detach and protect myself. She was shocked and perceived it as a cruel, intentional punishment.

As the months of our separate living passed by, I continued to pray for guidance. I repeatedly felt I should not rush to file for divorce but that I should "wait for the Lord."

*Wait on the Lord, and keep his way, and he shall*
*exalt thee to inherit the land. (Psalm 37:34)*

After about four months of separation, I was at work one day and the receptionist came to my office in a panic, saying that a "crazy woman" was yelling on the phone demanding to talk to me. It was Helen's sister calling to tell me Helen had fallen and twisted around in her bathtub and that her small leg had been shattered. She was going to be in the hospital, and the surgeons would do what they could.

I knew this could be a catastrophe for Helen. I decided to make the trip to Pennsylvania and drove into the night to get to her hospital room around 2:00 a.m. I dreaded what I might experience there.

To my astonishment, she smiled serenely as I walked in. I couldn't believe her calm state of mind. She told me the doctors had already surgically implanted metal bars in her leg, hoping it would become functional again.

As I tried to sleep later that night, an impression seeped in that we might get back together again, somehow. I allowed for that thought to remain but held it at arm's length, with severe caution.

With skilled doctors, prayers of faith, and the laying on of hands, she began to walk. Though never as well as before, she could at least walk again. Within a couple of years, however, she had to use a wheelchair whenever we went outside.

Ultimately, this experience was beneficial for Helen. During her recovery, we were still separated and she was stuck alone in the house with little help. Then amazingly, God sent our teenage nephew to live with her and help her, which was truly a miracle in terms of timing. Helen still felt the weight of caring for herself and—without me around—there was nobody to blame for whatever was happening.

The harsh realities of life seemed to close in on her, facilitating God's treatment plan and personal tutoring. Had Helen not believed I was pursuing a divorce, she would not have felt fully responsible to act for herself and come face-to-face with her own fears, thoughts, and habits.

She started listening to religious programming on TV, its inspiring messages filling her with hope. Today she testifies that for the first time, she began to live with faith and put the Lord first. She lost weight because nobody fed her, she would joke, but in truth, she followed a strict diet and quit taking all her weight-gain-inducing medications (which is not something we recommend doing independently).

And so it was that a perplexing prompting to pursue divorce led to progress in Helen's life and ultimately, a stronger union.

After a few months of talking by phone, I could sense the difference in her and naively assumed everything would be better now that the gospel had truly come into her life. *Perhaps the meds weren't necessary after all*, I thought. But quite soon she would need medications again.

We agreed to reunite, and that was our last separation (nineteen years ago as of this writing).

## Breaking the Eggshells

As with the other separations, growth had occurred for both of us, and our relationship was functioning better than before. But our problems came back with intensity.

We bought another house near my job and moved in with high hopes and a few enthusiastic, peace-filled weeks together.

But gradually, she started to act a bit like "the old Helen." What was going on? Why? We were both so optimistic, trying so hard.

For the first time, I began to understand that I was a significant part of the problem. I was somehow triggering her upsets. In many ways, she had been living in greater peace without me. And she was getting more upset the longer we were together! What was I doing wrong?

This was all deeply concerning. "Were we not meant to be, after all?" But I had received powerful witnesses from the Holy Spirit that we were right for each other and should get back together again.

With some horror, I also noticed I was changing mentally too. I was slowing down a little and wasn't able to handle her behaviors as well as before. I was more easily fatigued, and that concerned me.

One day, Helen was yelling something at me—probably a no-win situation of some kind where I felt trapped by her conflicting directions. I recall reflexively ducking behind a recliner in our living room as she hollered from the other side of the room.

It wasn't until after I had left the room that I realized what I had done. I had ducked behind the chair to shield myself from her words! I was afraid of her. I was terrified that the abuse would never end.

Reflecting on that incident later, I also feared I was being permanently harmed psychologically. Who on earth hides behind a chair during an argument?

Around this time, I discovered the book *Stop Walking on Eggshells*, which I strongly recommend for anyone living with a person with BPD. I began to understand how, when, and why a person with BPD is triggered. This book satisfied my deep need to understand what on earth was happening and how to prevent or minimize Helen's outbursts. (This illustrates why we so strongly recommend that you learn about your spouse's condition or illness and seek the guidance of mental health professionals. For your sake, you need to understand what's going on.)

I also realized that I had been unintentionally triggering painful emotional upsets for Helen. I understood why, in some ways, she had been happier living alone. I now knew better what *not* to do and say. I saw that my efforts to fix or prevent problems were misguided and harmful. I meant well, but I was not helping. I lacked understanding.

I gradually began to do better but monitoring my words and facial expressions while watching out for her feelings and mental state were draining on me. And it is impossible to prevent *all* conflict, despite our best efforts, even today.

## My Near Collapse

I was so broken by the stress of our relationship, I hesitantly suggested we sleep in separate beds. I was surprised when she agreed, and I credit a merciful God with helping us both see the necessity of it.

For many years previous, whenever Helen was upset, she would fuss with me incessantly, even after we went to bed. This was her most dreaded, destructive behavior because she would wake me up as soon as I fell asleep. If she was still steaming mad, I wasn't going to have the pleasure of falling asleep. "You have to get me out of this!" she would often say.

I would just lie there as still as I could and try not to snore. It was traumatizing because in my near-subconscious state, she would be there again, saying awful things. This happened quite often for over fifteen *years*.

It took seven years of sleeping separately before I felt safe enough to sleep next to her again, and even then, I was nervous for weeks.

At the lowest point in my life, the mental fatigue was so intense I was pretty much in a depression for three years straight. My mental health professionals could not find the right medications; nothing helped.

But somehow, miraculously, Helen became very gentle with me. Not all the time, but sometimes. She allowed me to be weak and vulnerable. She exhibited saintly kindness and patience, which I craved and appreciated beyond words. She let me fully express myself and share how upset and hurt I was without having a meltdown herself. This was unheard of in earlier years. I can still picture several settings where such conversations took place. One time, I cried my eyes out while she just sat silently, hand on my back, occasionally saying things like, "It's okay. Go ahead. I know it's been really hard on you."

The relief was inexpressible.

I thank God for giving me an easy job during that time. I was so worn out I could not have handled anything more. I worked with kind and caring people who were having similar life experiences. God is so merciful. He has always given me what is needed—even if He doesn't fully take the problem away.

That same year, doctors finally diagnosed my mental illness and found the right combination of medications to help me feel better. Bipolar disorder 2 is often misdiagnosed as clinical depression, they told me, and they confirmed that I had bipolar disorder 2. Today, I feel amazing most of the time, thanks to spiritual learning and healing, my medications, and a much more stable relationship with Helen.

## Blessings from within the Furnace

Problems and hard times are often called the "furnace of affliction." The problems may hurt terribly, but the intensity of the flame does positive things to our souls—if we accept those problems with faith in God.

I recall often thinking to myself, *Am I being destroyed by all these problems? Is my life being ruined?*

The answer was always no.

Deficits resulting from my drug-using years, character flaws, and poor social skills were gradually being addressed. *I'm better off now than I was before I met Helen*, I often remember thinking.

Her personality and strengths were indispensable to building my self-confidence. She drew so much out of me that just wasn't there before. Her innate talents, humor, energy, social skills, and love of children and domestic things brought us a great deal of joy, even throughout the terrible trials.

I had better jobs over time. I was effective at work and respected. Sure, there were hard days, but I was generally considered a solid, sometimes exceptional employee.

I was maturing in my knowledge of God and beginning to reflect more of His character. I could feel the foolishness being burned out of my soul, and I was spiritually maturing.

*Many are the afflictions of the righteous: but the Lord*
*delivereth him out of them all. (Psalm 34:17-20)*

## Dialectical Behavior Therapy

Nevertheless, some hard times continued for another six years after I was diagnosed and properly medicated. I had more strength to cope with the troubles, so it took less of a toll on me, but it was still highly disruptive and Helen was extremely volatile at times.

Of course, throughout all of these hard times from the earliest days of our marriage, there were many, many truly enjoyable good times and wonderful memories made. Nobody should imagine we experienced twenty-plus years of endless misery. But as of yet, we still hadn't been able to exit that dysfunctional rollercoaster ride. Round and round we went.

In 2012, she ended up in a psychiatric hospital again in a terrible, angry state, but it led to the most important, life-changing opportunity of our life.

The key to Helen's lasting and deep change was her decision to attend a three-month, full-time treatment program in Pittsburgh focused on dialectical behavior therapy (DBT), which is considered the most effective form of therapy for individuals with my wife's conditions. We had to move to Pittsburgh temporarily so that she could attend the program from 9 a.m. to 5 p.m., five days a week. This was costly and highly inconvenient, but we knew it was a priceless opportunity. We decided it was worth the effort and prayed it would work. Tragically, Helen was there with an open mind and eager to learn while most participants were court-committed, required to attend, and had no interest in learning anything all.

DBT therapy *"aims to build mindfulness, distress tolerance, emotion regulation and distress tolerance skills."*[1] In simpler terms, DBT helps the person manage their thoughts and feelings using specific techniques.

Helen had many unreasonable thinking and communication habits she believed were normal and other people should accept. Her participation in this program "popped a lot of bubbles," as tactless participants in the program blasted her logic and criticized her.

Afterwards, counselors patched things up, helping Helen understand her negative patterns and learn better ways to handle stressful situations. Every night we debriefed what she had experienced. She nearly quit during her first two weeks but thankfully, she began to feel better and became fully committed—and happier.

While Helen was in this DBT program, doctors placed her on new medications for her bipolar disorder, which still require adjustment sometimes. She still needs to participate in therapy from time to time, which brings those DBT skills back into focus and helps her avoid sliding into destructive thought patterns.

# Joyful, After All

Today, Helen and I experience joy and peace in our marriage. I believe we are both more Christlike because of our experiences. We still have occasional-to-frequent tensions—severe at times—but discussions about differences of opinion are generally calm, and our marriage continues to be a God-inspired union that blesses us and others.

Looking back at our gut-wrenching experiences, we can see that God really did know what was best.

## Scripture to Ponder:

*"For My thoughts are not your thoughts, neither are your ways My ways," declares the LORD. "For as the heavens are higher than the earth, so are My ways higher than your ways, and My thoughts than your thoughts" (Isaiah 55:8-9)*

# Appendix B
# Recommended Resources

This appendix contains carefully selected, valuable resources, most of which you've already previewed in the chapters of this book.

The free online resources below have all sorts of helpful information about specific mental health conditions and the prevalence of mental health issues in the United States alone.

## Free online resources

### Brief Descriptions of Mental Health Conditions

From the National Alliance on Mental Illness, this free resource is well organized, comprehensive, and easy to understand: https://www.nami.org/Learn-More/Mental-Health-Conditions

### Statistics: Occurrence of Mental Health Issues in the United States

https://www.nami.org/learn-more/mental-health-by-the-numbers

### Domestic Violence and Abuse: Detailed Descriptions, Support Resources, and Recommendations from The Hotline

https://www.thehotline.org/is-this-abuse/abuse-defined/

### SAMHSA (Substance Abuse and Mental Health Services Administration)

From the U.S. Department of Health and Human Services, this website has a host of resources specifically for family members of the mentally ill and addicted. Hotline number and complete listing of resources are found here: https://www.samhsa.gov/find-help/national-helpline

### Christian-based "Celebrate Recovery," a 12-Step Program

Worldwide program founded by pastor and author Rick Warren. View their homepage to find locations near you, primarily for substance abuse and other compulsive behaviors: https://www.celebraterecovery.com/

## BOOKS AVAILABLE FOR PURCHASE

| # | Book Title and Author(s) | Why We Recommend It |
|---|---|---|
| 1 | *The Meaning of Marriage: Facing the Complexities of Commitment with the Wisdom of God*<br><br>by Timothy Keller and Kathy Keller | *The Meaning of Marriage* is listed first for a reason. Most of us today hold incorrect notions about marriage. This book gets to the heart of God's view of marriage and how it is supposed to work. You won't realize how many marital landmines have been planted around you through the influence of our culture until you read this book.<br><br>With compelling stories and eye-opening statistics, this book imparts biblical wisdom every married couple should understand before they even start dating. But it's not too late to learn. We wish we could go back and give this book to our sixteen-year-old selves.<br><br>While *Healing the Stormy Marriage* is written for spouses in unstable relationships, *The Meaning of Marriage* addresses fundamentals that apply to every marriage. |

Learn more:

| # | Book Title and Author(s) | Why We Recommend It |
|---|---|---|
| 2 | *The 5 Love Languages: The Secret to Love that Lasts* <br><br> by Gary D. Chapman | This short yet powerful book is an easy read that clears up misunderstandings about how spouses want to receive love and how they often think they're great at giving love—but are often mistaken. <br><br> Even with the best of intentions, we often don't realize what makes our spouse tick in terms of giving and receiving love. This book provides concrete, actionable advice that can make an enormous difference in our relationships. |

Learn more:

| # | Book Title and Author(s) | Why We Recommend It |
|---|---|---|
| 3 | *The Seven Principles for Making Marriage Work: A Practical Guide from the Country's Foremost Relationship Expert* by John Gottman and Nan Silver | The amazing research of these authors enables them to predict with 90 percent-plus accuracy whether a married couple will divorce. Astonishing but true. This book helps spouses avoid the marriage-crushing behaviors that lead to divorce by teaching the opposite behaviors—the seven principles that have been consistently demonstrated to produce happy marriages. The book makes consummate sense, is easy to read, and is full of memorable stories and motivation to do better. |

Learn more:

| # | Book Title and Author(s) | Why We Recommend It |
|---|---|---|
| 4 | *Key Core Beliefs: Unlocking the HEART of Happiness & Health* by H. Gray Otis, Sandi Williams, and James Messina | This outstanding, practical resource will help you understand and improve your deepest level of consciousness, including your beliefs about yourself and your emotions. This book cleared up so many mysteries for me—particularly related to emotional tangles—that it is impossible to overstate its value. It will help you understand what is going on in your mind and heart as you interact with your spouse and others. You will gain subtle but important insights into how your behaviors may be affecting your spouse. You will learn techniques for improving communication that can dramatically decrease negative feelings and stress. |

Learn more:

| # | Book Title and Author(s) | Why We Recommend It |
|---|---|---|
| 5 | *Jesus Calling: Enjoying Peace in His Presence,* deluxe edition with the pink cover (*Jesus Calling®*)<br><br>by Sarah Young<br><br>There are many editions available. This is the classic. | This book promotes a connection to God in a way like no other book I have found (other than scripture).<br><br>People who are suffering will particularly benefit because it helps the reader rise above the chaos and pain of life and find greater peace through a moment-by-moment connection to Christ.<br><br>This book has sold millions of copies, and I have given it as a cherished gift to others. Do yourself a favor and strengthen your connection to Christ with this inspired resource comprising brief daily readings (five minutes, plus prayer and pondering). |

Learn more:

| # | Book Title and Author(s) | Why We Recommend It |
|---|---|---|
| 6 | *Jesus Christ, His Life and Mine: The Story of Jesus and How It Applies to Us in the Twitter Era*<br><br>by R. Christian Bohlen | It is difficult to comprehend what it means to follow Jesus's example in our marriages if we are not intimately familiar with His earthly life.<br><br>This easy, engaging read promotes a rich understanding of the character of Jesus and how to apply His example and teachings to modern situations. It is like a guided tour with a caring mentor who knows the culture and language of Jesus's day.<br><br>When we face tough times, we need the Light of Christ to fill our hearts. Nothing does that more effectively than reading the entire birth-to-resurrection story of Jesus with a believing heart. There is a power that fills the soul that cannot be obtained in any other way. |

Learn more:

# End Notes

All scripture citations are from the King James Version (KJV) unless otherwise noted. Note that quotation marks have been added to scripture citations from the KJV, where necessary, to create a consistent reading experience with the more modern Bible translations also used in this book:

ESV – English Standard Version

NIV – New International Version

NKJV – New King James Version

NLT – New Living Translation

## Introduction

1.  "What is Mental Illness?" American Psychiatric Association, accessed April 28, 2021, https://www.psychiatry.org/patients-families/what-is-mental-illness.

2.  "5 Surprising Mental Health Statistics," MentalHealthFirstAid. org, accessed April 28, 2021, https://www.mentalhealthfirstaid. org/2019/02/5-surprising-mental-health-statistics/; (see also "Mental Health by the Numbers," NAMI.org at https://www. nami.org/mhstats).

3.  Francis Chan and Leah Chan, *You and Me Forever: Marriage in Light of Eternity* (Sandy Croft: Claire Love Publishing, 2014), Introduction, Kindle.

4.  R. Christian Bohlen, "My Story," accessed April 28, 2021, https://rchristianbohlen.com/how-christ-found-me/.

5.  Hindu proverb, accessed August 5, 2019, http://www.quotationspage.com/quote/36407.html.

## Chapter 1: I'm So Confused

1.  Robert Fulghum, *True Love: Stories Told to and By Robert Fulghum*, (New York: HarperCollins Publishers, 1997), 96–98; note: this quotation is often incorrectly attributed to Dr. Suess.

2.  Denis de Rougemont, *Love in the Western World* (New York: Harper and Row, 1956), 300; quoted in Timothy Keller and Kathy Keller, *The Meaning of Marriage: Facing the Complexities of Commitment with the Wisdom of God* (London: Penguin Books, reprint edition), chapter 1, Kindle.

## Chapter 2: How Can I Start Feeling Like Myself Again?

1.  "Power and Control: Break Free from Abuse," TheHotline.org, accessed April 28, 2021, https://www.thehotline.org/identify-abuse/power-and-control/.

2.  "What Emotional Abuse Really Means," OneLove.org, accessed April 28, 2021, https://www.joinonelove.org/learn/emotional-abuse-really-means/.

3.  "The Power and Danger of Disconnecting from Ourselves," ManhattanMentalHealthCounseling.com, accessed August 21, 2020, https://manhattanmentalhealthcounseling.com/the-power-and-danger-of-disconnecting-from-ourselves/.

4. H. Gray Otis, Sandi Williams, and James Messina, *Key Core Beliefs: Unlocking the HEART of Happiness & Health* (Highland: Colorian Press, 2018) chapter 10, Kindle. See also Tara Brach's outstanding book, *Radical Compassion* (London: Penguin Life, 2019).

5. "What is Emotional Intelligence?" *Psychology Today*, accessed April 28, 2021, https://www.psychologytoday.com/us/basics/emotional-intelligence.

## Chapter 3: I'm Starting to Doubt Myself and My Faith

1. Janice Cauwels, *Imbroglio: Rising to the Challenges of Borderline Personality Disorder* (New York: W. W. Norton, 1992), quoted in Paul Mason and Randi Kreger, *Stop Walking on Eggshells: Taking Your Life Back When Someone You Care About Has Borderline Personality Disorder* (Oakland: New Harbinger Publications, 2010).

2. A. J. Mahari, a BPD taken from the non-BPD internet support group, quoted in Mason and Kreger, *Stop Walking on Eggshells*, 53.

3. Paul T. T. Mason and Randi Kreger, *Stop Walking on Eggshells: Taking Your Life Back When Someone You Care About Has Borderline Personality Disorder* (Oakland: New Harbinger Publications), 13.

4. Jim Stout and Leah Stout, *Mental Illness and Your Marriage: Surviving, Healing, and Rebuilding* (self-published, 2017), chapter 4, Kindle.

5. Thomas S. Monson, "Finding Joy in the Journey," accessed April 28, 2021, https://www.churchofjesuschrist.org/study/general-conference/2008/10/finding-joy-in-the-journey?lang=eng.

6.  "Personal boundaries," Wikipedia, accessed August 10, 2019, https://en.wikipedia.org/wiki/Personal_boundaries.

7.  R. Christian Bohlen, "My Story," accessed April 28, 2021, https://rchristianbohlen.com/how-christ-found-me/.

8.  Jim Stout, *Abandoned and Betrayed by God: Surviving a Crisis of Faith* (San Antonio: Shepherd Publishing, 2016), part 2, Guidelines 1–15, Kindle.

9.  Roland Bainton, *Here I Stand* (New York and Nashville: Abingdon- Cokesbury Press, 1950), 361, quoted in M. Vernon Begalke, "Luther's Anfechtungen: An Important Clue to His Pastoral Theology," *Consensus*: vol. 8, no. 3 (1982): article 1, accessed April 28, 2021, http://scholars.wlu.ca/consensus/vol8/iss3/1.

10. Erin Ramachandran, *Mental Health Strong: A Christian's Guide to Walking Resiliently alongside Your Spouse with a Mental Health Condition* (Bloomington: iUniverse, 2019), prologue, Kindle. This award-winning book includes an extensive listing of resources for spouses and family members affected by mental health issues.

## Chapter 4: Can I Survive This?

1.  See https://www.joinonelove.org/learn/emotional-abuse-really-means/ and https://www.thehotline.org/is-this-abuse/abuse-defined/, and https://reachma.org/6-different-types-abuse/ for more information, accessed April 28, 2021.

2.  John Gottman and Nan Silver, *The Seven Principles for Making Marriage Work: A Practical Guide from the Country's Foremost Relationship Expert* (New York: Random House, 2015), chapter 2, Kindle.

3. Gottman and Silver, *The Seven Principles for Making Marriage Work*, chapter 2, Kindle.

4. Timothy Keller and Kathy Keller, *The Meaning of Marriage: Facing the Complexities of Commitment with the Wisdom of God* (New York: Dutton, 2011), chapter 3, Kindle.

5. Keller and Keller, *The Meaning of Marriage*, chapter 3, Kindle.

6. Keller and Keller, *The Meaning of Marriage*, chapter 3, Kindle; see also "Should Couples in Unhappy Marriages Stay Together?" IFStudies.org, accessed April 28, 2021, https://ifstudies.org/blog/should-couples-in-unhappy-marriages-stay-together.

## Chapter 5: It's Not Fair

1. Russell M. Nelson, "Joy and Spiritual Survival," https://www.churchofjesuschrist.org/study/general-conference/2016/10/joy-and-spiritual-survival?lang=eng. Accessed April 28, 2021.

2. Stephen R. Covey, *The 7 Habits of Highly Effective People: Powerful Lessons in Personal Change* (New York: RosettaBooks, 2013), Kindle.

3. This quote is often attributed to Mohandas K. Ghandi, but there are many before him who made similar statements. The exact origin of "Be the change you wish to see in the world" is still unclear. See the full research here, accessed April 28, 2021: https://quoteinvestigator.com/2017/10/23/be-change/.

## Chapter 6: My Needs Are Not Being Met

1. Abraham H. Maslow, "A Theory of Human Motivation," *Psychological Review*, 50 (1943) 4: 370–96, accessed April 28, 2021, citation found at: http://psychclassics.yorku.ca/author.htm#m.

2.  Gordon B. Hinckley, "Whosoever Will Save His Life," accessed April 28, 2021, https://www.churchofjesuschrist.org/study/ensign/1982/08/whosoever-will-save-his-life?lang=eng.

3.  Morris Kline, *Mathematics in Western Culture* (New York: Oxford University Press, 1953).

4.  H. Gray Otis, Sandi Williams, and James Messina, *Key Core Beliefs: Unlocking the HEART of Happiness & Health* (Highland: Colorian Press, 2018), chapter 10, Kindle.

5.  Rick Warren, *The Purpose Driven Life: What On Earth Am I Here For?*, expanded edition (Grand Rapids: Zondervan, 2011), 229.

6.  Sherri Stritof, "10 Things Women Want From Their Husbands," Verywellmind, https://www.verywellmind.com/what-women-want-from-husbands-2303313., accessed August 6, 2019.

7.  Sherri Stritof, "10 Things Men Want From Their Wives," https://www.verywellmind.com/what-men-want-from-their-wives-2303311., accessed August 6, 2019.

8.  Gary D. Chapman, *The 5 Love Languages: The Secret to Love That Lasts*, (Chicago: Northfield Publishing, 2015), chapter 2, Kindle.

9.  Chapman, *The 5 Love Languages*, chapter 1, Kindle.

10. Chapman, *The 5 Love Languages*, chapter 7, Kindle.

11. "Thrive," Dictionary.com, accessed April 28, 2021, https://www.dictionary.com/browse/thrive (for synonyms, see also https://www.thesaurus.com/browse/thrive).

12. Melody Beattie, *Codependent No More: How to Stop Controlling Others and Start Caring for Yourself* (Center City: Hazelden Publishing, 1986).

13. Sarah Young, *Jesus Calling: Enjoying Peace in His Presence*, deluxe edition, pink cover (Nashville: Thomas Nelson, 2013), November 2 entry, Kindle.

14. Donald DeMarco, "The Virtue of Chastity," Catholic Exchange, accessed April 28, 2021, https://catholicexchange.com/the-virtue-of-chastity.

15. Keller and Keller, *The Meaning of Marriage*, chapter 2, Kindle.

## Chapter 7: I'm Totally Drained and Afraid

1. James L. Farrell, *The Peacegiver* (Salt Lake City: Deseret Book, 2004), chapter 5, Kindle.

2. Keller and Keller, *The Meaning of Marriage*, chapter 2, Kindle.

3. "4100 Pisteuo," Strong's Exhaustive Concordance on Bible Hub, accessed on April 28, 2021, https://biblehub.com/strongs/greek/4100.htm.

4. See John 15:5; Psalm 34:8; Nahum 1:7; Psalm 84:11.

5. Rick Warren Quotes. BrainyQuote.com, BrainyMedia Inc, https://www.brainyquote.com/quotes/rick_warren_599793, accessed April 28, 2021.

## Chapter 8: My Spouse is Walking All Over Me!

1. Henry Cloud and John Townsend, *Boundaries: When to Say Yes, How to Say No to Take Control of Your Life*, expanded and updated Edition (Grand Rapids: Zondervan, 2017), chapter 2, Kindle.

2. James Emery White, "Is God a Moral Monster? The Slaughter of the Canaanites," accessed April 28, 2021, https://www.churchandculture.org/blog/2020/10/22/is-god-a-moral-monster.

3. Cloud and Townsend, *Boundaries*, chapter 2, Kindle.

4. Cloud and Townsend, *Boundaries*, chapter 2, Kindle.

5. John Piper, *Don't Waste Your Life, Group Study Edition* (Wheaton: Crossway Books, 2007), 107.

6. Cloud and Townsend, *Boundaries*, chapter 5, Kindle.

7. Cloud and Townsend, *Boundaries*, chapter 4, Kindle.

8. John Gottman and Nan Silver, *The Seven Principles for Making Marriage Work: A Practical Guide from the Country's Foremost Relationship Expert* (New York: Harmony Books, 2015), chapter 2, Kindle.

9. Gottman and Silver, *The Seven Principles for Making Marriage Work*, chapter 11, Kindle.

10. Gottman and Silver, *The Seven Principles for Making Marriage Work*, chapter 11, Kindle.

11. Cloud and Townsend, *Boundaries*, chapter 15, Kindle.

## Chapter 9: I Can't Plan Anything

1. Sarah Young, *Jesus Calling*, January 16 reading.

2. Jeffrey Brantley and Jon Kabat-Zinn, *Calming Your Anxious Mind: How Mindfulness and Compassion Can Free You from Anxiety, Fear, and Panic* (Oakland: New Harbinger Publications, 2007).

3. "Definition of patience in English," Lexico, accessed April 28, 2021, https://www.lexico.com/en/definition/patience.

4. Sarah Young, *Jesus Calling*, November 10 reading.

5. "Prayer for Serenity," Celebrate Recovery: A Christ-Centered 12 Step Program, accessed April 28, 2021, https://www.celebraterecovery.com/resources/cr-tools/serenityprayer.

## Chapter 10: My Heart Breaks for My Spouse.

1. Keller and Keller, *The Meaning of Marriage*, chapter 1, Kindle.

2. Stout and Stout, *Mental Illness and Your Marriage*, chapter 4, Kindle.

## Chapter 11: My Hopes for My Life Are Unraveling

1. Gottman and Silver, *The Seven Principles for Making Marriage Work*, chapter 11, Kindle.

2. Otis, Williams, and Messina, *Key Core Beliefs*, chapter 10, Kindle.

## Chapter 12: Happy After All

1. "Three Things Fear Does to Relationships," PastorRick, accessed April 28, 2021, https://pastorrick.com/three-things-fear-does-to-relationships/.

2. "How Many Times Does the Bible Say 'Fear Not,'" WordNuggets, accessed April 28, 2021, https://wordnuggets.wordpress.com/2009/03/02/how-many-times-does-the-bible-say-fear-not/.

3. Mason and Kreger, *Stop Walking on Eggshells*, 110.

4. Mason and Kreger, *Stop Walking on Eggshells*, 110.

5. Lexico, powered by Oxford, "Surrender," accessed April 28, 2021, https://www.lexico.com/en/definition/surrender.

## Appendix A: Our Story

1. "Mental Health Basics: dialectical behavior therapy," Eluna, accessed August 5, 2019, https://elunanetwork.org/resources/mental-health-basics-dialectical-behavior-therapy/.